Next Line, Please

Next Line, Please

Prompts to Inspire Poets and Writers

EDITED BY
David Lehman

WITH
Angela Ball

FOREWORD BY
Robert Wilson

Cornell University Press
Ithaca and London

First published 2018 by Cornell University Press

Printed in the United States of America

Library of Congress Cataloging-in-Publication Data

Names: Lehman, David, 1948– editor. | Ball, Angela,
    1952– editor.
Title: Next line, please : prompts to inspire poets and writers /
    edited by David Lehman with Angela Ball ; foreword by
    Robert Wilson.
Description: Ithaca : Cornell University Press, 2018. |
    Includes index.
Identifiers: LCCN 2017038718 (print) | LCCN 2017041802
    (ebook) | ISBN 9781501715150 (epub/mobi) |
    ISBN 9781501715501 (pdf) | ISBN 9781501715006 |
    ISBN 9781501715006 (pbk. : alk. paper)
Subjects: LCSH: American poetry—21st century. | American
    poetry—21st century—History and criticism. | Poetry—
    Authorship—Collaboration.
Classification: LCC PS617 (ebook) | LCC PS617 .N495 2018
    (print) | DDC 808.1—dc23
LC record available at https://lccn.loc.gov/2017038718

Cornell University Press strives to use environmentally
responsible suppliers and materials to the fullest extent possible
in the publishing of its books. Such materials include vegetable-
based, low-VOC inks and acid-free papers that are recycled,
totally chlorine-free, or partly composed of nonwood fibers. For
further information, visit our website at cornellpress.cornell.edu.

Contents

Angela Ball wrote the entries from June 23, 2015, through September 29, 2015; David Lehman composed the rest.

Acknowledgments

Heartfelt thanks to Robert Wilson, Bruce Falconer, and Margaret Foster of *The American Scholar*; to Dean Smith and the editorial team at Cornell University Press; to Ange Romeo-Hall, our editor at the Press; to Dina Dineva, who made this book's index; to my literary agent, Glen Hartley; to Angela Ball for her indispensable contributions to this book; to Thomas Moody and Virginia Valenzuela for their assistance; and to my wife, Stacey Lehman, source of many prompts and much inspiration.

Foreword
Robert Wilson

We wanted to have a department on our website that regularly featured poetry, which we print in each issue of *The American Scholar* itself. But we thought, for the web, our approach should be different. We also wanted to connect with what we know is an enthusiastic but often ignored universe of people who write poetry without necessarily expecting to be published and acclaimed. From these thoughts came the idea of crowd-sourced poetry and then the notion that our online readers would write a poem line by line, week by week. It would be a contest for the best or most appropriate line each week. And from there came the title, "Next Line, Please."

That should have been the easy part, and finding the right person to make it happen should have been the hard part. We needed someone whose choice of the winning line each week would be authoritative. But we also wanted someone who would enter into the spirit of the contest—more quiz-show host than grader of homework. Someone who takes fun seriously and could make serious work seem like fun.

Our first choice was always David Lehman. A brilliant poet himself, the longtime editor of the *Best American Poetry* series, a teacher, a fine prose writer—someone whom we had often published. And a fellow with a touch of the showman in him, who had written one book about the American songbook and was writing another about Frank Sinatra. As an added benefit, I had known David long enough to remember when he wrote for *Newsweek,* so there was no concern about his making a weekly deadline.

Lucky for us, we never had to come up with a second choice. David loved the idea and accepted it without reservation. He saw right away that this experiment in poetry writing would require an enthusiastic and energetic ringmaster, and from the first column he got the tone just right. What David added, which we had not imagined or requested, was a brief but valuable lesson each week on poetic form or technique or history.

When the first sonnet was completed, after our audience built it a line a week for thirteen weeks (David had offered the first line himself), and the title "Monday" had been chosen, I heard from a friend who had watched the process without himself participating. He said he was amazed by just what a fine poem "Monday" had turned out to be. The friend happened to have once won a Pulitzer Prize for distinguished criticism, so this was praise that itself felt authoritative.

We ourselves liked what David and our readers—*his* readers—were doing. Our admiration for him grew week by week, for his erudition, his wit, his unflagging enthusiasm and, well, his leadership. He had created a merry online poetic band. At some point David let us know that he was having health problems. We offered what support we could: take time off, or skip a week if you don't feel like doing it. Eventually, when he had a major operation, the poet Angela Ball ably replaced him for a while. But except for those recovery months, David kept turning in his flawless copy each week, never hinting to his audience what he was going through, never presenting anything but his always upbeat and encouraging self. We hadn't known that our admiration for him could grow. But it did.

Next Line, Please

Introduction

David Lehman

This was Robert Wilson's idea. Bob is the editor of *The American Scholar*, the "general readership" quarterly of the Phi Beta Kappa Society. It is his business to come up with ideas for columns and magazine "departments," and he is very good at devising such features. In April 2014, he asked whether I would serve as quizmaster of "Next Line, Please," a weekly online poetry competition that would run on the magazine's website. "You would pick a kind of poem you'd like to see written," he said. "We've been thinking of starting with a sonnet, just because it's such a familiar form, but it's really up to you. You'd then write a pretty brief intro explaining the overall concept and then the particular requirements for the form you choose. This intro would continue to run until the poem is done. You'd come up with the first line. We'd have a bit of text below explaining how readers can offer a suggested line."

Game as I am for competitions, contests, and challenges that end in collaborative poems, I said yes without hesitation. The magazine then issued a press release:

NEXT LINE, PLEASE
Help us write a sonnet

On Tuesday, May 6, *The American Scholar* will launch a website experiment in writing crowd-sourced poetry—in this case, a Shakespearean sonnet.

David Lehman, the series editor for *The Best American Poetry* volumes, has provided the first line for the sonnet, and will solicit a new line from our web audience each week. Lehman will pick finalists and a winner on the subsequent week, and readers will be encouraged to comment on his choice of the winning line.

Please join us for what we hope will be an amusing and enlightening poetic undertaking, and encourage all the poets and would-be poets you know to try their hand at "Next Line, Please."

Lehman's first line: *How like a prison is my cubicle*

Look for Lehman's introduction and our instructions on Tuesday, May 6, at: theamericanscholar.org/nextline

And remember to check back each Tuesday to watch the sonnet grow.

And we were off.

"Next Line, Please" began as a competition and its novelty drew immediate interest. We went from line to line and, reading all the columns in a row in this book, you can see how we built the sonnet, brick by brick, the stanza divisions emerging toward the end, the title affixed as the finishing stroke. In three months we had written a publishable sonnet and chronicled our doing so, and what pleased me most was the variety and range of individuals who joined that "we." We comprised two well-known professors (Leo Braudy, Sandra M. Gilbert), two published poets (Frank Bidart, Laura Cronk), and a composer (Lewis Saul). We also included four persons about whom one could only conjecture because they represented themselves with pen names (MQ, Diana, James the Lesser, Jamie). Two winners of the weekly competitions were previously unknown to me (Anna E. Moss, Katie Whitney), and line three of the sonnet was the contribution of "Brian Anderson and his twelfth-grade composition class."

The exercise facilitated an escape from the world of professional poets. We had gone beyond the usual bounds in providing a space for poetry to exist as a collective endeavor and a collective pleasure, one that includes the university but is not limited to it. The pen names supplied evidence in favor of a view I have long held: that pseudonyms, personae, and masks are a legitimate way to liberate the imagination from the shackles of the superego.

After we completed the sonnet, "Next Line, Please" continued, so it seemed, on its own momentum. Never forgetting that our overriding aim was what Wordsworth called "the grand elementary principle of pleasure," I found myself in the role of instructor explaining or commenting on certain forms (the haiku, the tanka, the sestina, the limerick, the cento, the two-line poem) and introducing other strategies for writing poetry. We didn't always proceed line by line, as with our sonnets, or stanza by stanza, as with our sestina, although there have been times when the poems submitted one week provided the prompts for the next week. Each week I declared a first-place entry, a runner-up, and a bronze medal. When undecided between two entries, I might appeal to the community—we had become a community—to make the choice.

There are poets—Rilke was one—who wait years for inspiration to descend on them. But there is an alternative. I believe it is possible to create your own inspiration and that exercises of various sorts are indispensable for stimulating the imagination. Poets who subscribe to this view tend to give themselves assignments and, if they are teachers, they prepare such prompts for their students. To the extent that it constitutes an academic discipline, creative writing depends on these prompts. They may be traditional (write in a set form, imitate a poet) or improvised. Sometimes the spirit of competition is enough of a spur. Keats wrote the sonnet beginning "the poetry of earth is never dead" when he and his friend Leigh Hunt engaged in a friendly sonnet competition on the subject of the cricket and the grasshopper. Shelley wrote "Ozymandias" under a similar circumstance: dueling sonnets with his friend Horace Smith, using for a prompt a passage from the Greek historian Diodorus Siculus. To write a sonnet in, say, fifteen minutes can still serve as a parlor game or a class exercise, proof that the writing of serious poetry can start as an amusement—a word that embraces "muse."

Other prompts employ tricks to unlock the imagination. I borrowed "The Fake Apology" from William Carlos Williams's oft-anthologized "This Is Just to Say," in which the speaker begs his wife's forgiveness for eating the cold and delicious plums she may have been saving for breakfast. The speaker's delight in the plums implies that he's not sorry at all. And this is poetry's region, a land counter to fact, the land of the subjunctive mood. It is the region of possibility, dream, wish, falsehood, excuse, alibi, exaggeration, rumor. If it is an aspect of language that no statement can verify itself and that there is therefore nothing intrinsic to distinguish a sincere from an insincere statement, the poet can have a field day. And as the reader may infer from the previous sentence, the pedagogic ideas of Kenneth Koch, whose groundbreaking *Wishes, Lies, and Dreams* (1970) revolutionized the teaching of poetry in the schools, have been instrumental in forming my own view of how to do it.[1]

Asked to account for the success of our endeavor, as measured in the very appearance of this book and the anticipatory enthusiasm it has aroused, I would point to three things above all. One is the immediacy and spontaneity allowed by the Internet, which reduces and even eliminates the time between composition and publication. Some of the credit goes to the prompts. Completing an Emily Dickinson fragment is irresistible, it turns out, and the sestina is a form to which one can easily become addicted. I was thrilled, too, by the response to the call for couplets, the request that participants rewrite a passage of Milton's "Lycidas," and the directive to use the last line of Whitman's "Song of Myself" as the start of a new poem. But the lion's share of praise must go to the contributors, who took part with unflagging ardor and fertile imaginations.

"Next Line, Please" as a project and now as a book makes a case for poetry as an art that appeals to a general readership. We have demonstrated that it is possible to use digital means to create a lively and friendly club devoted to the pleasures of poetry. The pages that follow reflect the give-and-take among the contributors who commented on the posts each week. The "comments" space was always where participants posted their entries. It did not take too many months before contributors exchanged opinions, snark was notable in its absence, and the back-and-forth became a model of civil discourse. This level of exchange, this achievement of community, is remarkable at a time when we routinely encounter enormous amounts of rage and uncivil discourse perhaps especially on the net. The studious absence of politics helped.

[1] One of Koch's best early poems is a quartet of "variations" on the theme of Williams's "This Is Just to Say." In one of them the apologist, having broken the leg of the woman he took dancing, begs her forgiveness on the grounds that he "was clumsy" and wanted her "here in the wards, where I am the doctor!" The poem demonstrates that a good parody consists of equal amounts of appreciation and critique, that hostility can disguise itself in humor, and that the fake apology is one such disguise.

Our project acts toward politics as our parents suggested we should when they told us to avoid the subject at the dinner table. Nor is the association of dinner and poetry entirely fortuitous if poetry in its aspiration is, as I believe it is, a civilizing impulse, as well as, ideally, a source of amusement, pathos, wisdom, and wit, like the bardic tales told at a royal banquet or the performance of professional philosophers at a symposium on love.

In my posts I never mentioned that I was battling cancer when we initiated "Next Line, Please." During the time the contents of this book were written, I underwent procedures, treatments, more treatments, another procedure, a hospital stay. The sequence culminated in an aggressive regimen of chemotherapy followed by radical surgery. I saw no reason to broadcast the fact and every reason to keep quiet about it. The work of "Next Line, Please," in concert with the other work I was doing as a poet, writer, and editor, was helping to keep me alive. Work was my way of treating the disease—it was my creative escape, and the means by which I felt I could assert my continued existence in the world. In the summer of 2015, at the start of my recovery from major surgery, I asked the poet Angela Ball to take the helm of NLP. This she did wonderfully for the three months of my absence. I should add that Angela was and remains one of our regulars—she sets a very high bar with her submissions.

"Standing in for David as quizmaster was a revelation for me, an initiation into a special form of poetry as serious play," Angela reports. "The poet participants gamely produced spontaneous feats of language in response to every idea I threw out. One that drew some particularly fine entries was a 'product placement' prompt asking poets to include at least three existing or invented products in a new poem inspired by Kenneth Koch's brilliant poem 'You Were Wearing' (in which 'you' wore 'your Edgar Allan Poe printed cotton blouse' while father sported his 'Dick Tracy necktie'). As it happened, during my time heading the column, my partner of nine years very suddenly died, and 'Next Line, Please' became a vital respite and escape—collaboration and its energies a force field opposing despair. That my suggestions could inspire so much liveliness from people I had never encountered face-to-face was and is a lasting astonishment and balm."

This book contains most of the posts from May 2014 until the middle of October 2016. To bring the reader as close as possible to the present, we were obliged to omit some fifteen or so columns. Some of the posts have been lightly edited to avoid redundancy and for reasons of space. Can poetry thrive in the digital age? *Next Line, Please* answers in the affirmative. There is something magical about poetry, and though we think of the poet as working alone, working in the dark, it is all the better when a community of like-minded individuals emerges, sharing their joy in the written word.

Help Us Write a Sonnet: Line One

May 6, 2014

By David Lehman

"Next Line, Please" launches this week with a contest designed to pro-
duce a crowd-sourced sonnet. Each week we will add a line by free com-
petition; I will serve as judge. In my eyes it will be less a contest than a
collaboration, but it is undeniable that a prize structure has its attraction.
After all, it was in a sonnet competition that Shelley wrote "Ozymandias,"
perhaps his most frequently anthologized poem, ahead even of his "Ode
to the West Wind." If all goes well it should take approximately fifteen
weeks for us to craft the sonnet, with the final week devoted to picking a
title for it.

Originally imported from Italy, the sonnet is the most traditional of
English poetic forms. There were strict rules in the past, but in the era
of free verse the only requirement is that the poem must consist of four-
teen lines (and even this stricture has been challenged). In its heyday,
the Renaissance, glorious sonnet sequences were written by Shakespeare,
Spenser, Sidney, Wyatt, Surrey, and others. Traditional subjects include
love, beauty, time, death, the seasons, and how any two of these might
combine.

The sonnet has enjoyed other periods of glory. Wordsworth, Coleridge,
Shelley, and Keats made it a vehicle for the romantic impulse in English
poetry. Notable modern sonneteers range from Robert Frost to Edna
St. Vincent Millay. Emma Lazarus's "The New Colossus," the poem with
the stirring injunction that graces the Statue of Liberty, is a sonnet that
makes subtle allusions to Shelley's "Ozymandias."

The sonnet's fourteen lines can be distributed in several ways: in two
stanzas consisting of four lines each followed by two consisting of three
lines, for example, or in an eight-line stanza followed by a six-line stanza,
or in the same but without a line space separating the units. Shakespeare
favored three quatrains and a closing couplet. A characteristic rhyme

scheme is *abab,* though the *abba* pattern, in which one rhyme sandwiches another, has its champions, Tennyson and Auden among them.

The sonnet might begin with a comparison or a question—or sometimes both at once, as in the celebrated instance of Shakespeare's sonnet 18: "Shall I compare thee to a summer's day?" The subject is as much "you" as it is "summer," the first a metonymy for beauty, the second a metonymy for time. Poetry is the agency by which "thy eternal summer" may come into being, defeating the forces of death. "So long as men can breathe or eyes can see, / So long lives this, and this gives life to thee."

The poet may deploy the sonnet's lines strategically to advance an argument. It is crucial that the poem turn after the eighth line. This turn makes the structure of the sonnet apt for rhetorical ploys ranging from thesis and antithesis to theme-and-variation, generalization-and-exception, declaration followed by illustration. A qualifying conjunction, a "but" or a "yet," may initiate the sharp-toothed contrast.

I have written the first line of a sonnet in the Shakespearean manner. It is ten syllables and in pentameter (five poetic feet)—choices so out of keeping with current poetic practice that, in the spirit of contrarianism, I'd like to see contestants follow suit. I have left the end of the line unpunctuated in case my collaborators wish to extend the phrase. The trick is to surprise with word choice. If my first line works, it is because the last word in its pedestrianism differs strikingly from the nobility of the opening phrase.

How like a prison is my cubicle

Contestants may want to keep in mind that the paradox of liberty within imprisonment is used by Wordsworth in his sonnet about the sonnet form, "Nuns Fret Not at Their Convent's Narrow Room."

Help Us Write a Sonnet: Line Two

May 13, 2014

How like a prison is my cubicle
And yet how far my mind can freely roam

The many impressive second-line candidates left me undecided until the last moment when I opted for Leo Braudy's elegant "And yet how far my mind can freely roam." The succession of strong monosyllables broken only by the single crucial adverb won me over. Initially, I wondered at the wisdom of the turn signaled by the conjunction that begins the line; it seemed more appropriate for the pivot after line eight. On reflection, however, I thought it might be interesting to jump quickly to the paradox of freedom within constraints. It places a lot of pressure on the composers of lines three and four, which need to rhyme with "cubicle" and "roam" in any order.

My favorite runners-up include Lewis Saul's "While the boss smokes crack with his skanky whore," which would lead the poem in an entirely new and unexpected direction, and Matt Brogan's pun-filled "This pen of pens, this narrow bunk of bunk." I liked these so much that I even toyed with the idea of bifurcating the sonnet with alternative second lines.

Honorable mention goes to Amit Majmudar's alliterative submission: "I'm on the payroll, no prospect of parole." The doubtlessly pseudonymous Millicent Caliban deserves a commendation for the sturdy iambic line, "I can do naught but scroll, and type, and click." And Stacy (no last name given) came up with the fifth runner-up: "Where of my own volition I sit jailed."

One contestant wondered about the difficulty of rhyming with "cubicle." I fail to see the obstacle. I would also refer readers to a recent article in the *Wall Street Journal*. "When Office Cubicles Looked Like Progress" by Nikil Saval begins with the observation that "'Cubicle' has got to be one of the most efficient words in the English language. Nothing so swiftly conjures up a feeling of dread and drudgery." Saval, the author of *Cubed: A Secret History of the Workplace*, observes that the word "cubicle" appears in Richard Yates's great novel, *Revolutionary Road* (1961). Winston Smith reports to a cubicle each dreary day in Orwell's *1984*. The creator of the modern office cubicle, a designer named Robert Propst working for the office-furniture firm Herman Miller, had thought he was solving a major problem, that of the open office, not making a new one.

Help Us Write a Sonnet: Line Three

May 20, 2014

How like a prison is my cubicle
And yet how far my mind can freely roam
From gaol to Jerusalem, Hell to home

For the third verse in our group effort, I choose a line written by Brian Anderson and his twelfth-grade composition class.

I admit to a weakness for "gaol" spelled this way, and for works crafted communally, but I choose the line on the merits—attracted as I am by the antithesis and by the amount of ground, metaphysical and geographical, that the line covers.

The choice means that we are now committed to the *abba* stanza that Tennyson brought to perfection in his sequence of non-sonnets, "In Memoriam."

We had some excellent runners-up:

Melinda Wilson's play on Emily Dickinson, "Oh, in my brain, there is no funeral," leads the pack, followed by Eric Grace's "As, guided by a pharmaceutical." John Wark's "Unmade, mad, enclosed, endomed, whimsical" is as unusual as it is, well, whimsical, while Diana contributes a line of strong iambs, in which the strategic alternation of an "a" for an expected "the" caught my eye: "The sea, the waves, the air, a beach, the foam." Finally, I resisted Charles Marsh's clever lift of a line from Keats's "Ode to a Nightingale": "Through magic casements, opening on the foam." Keats's line differs in only one detail—the first word is "Charm'd," not "Through."

Please note that some candidates for line three will qualify for line four, which needs to rhyme with the dread "cubicle," so contestants should feel free to resubmit.

Help Us Write a Sonnet: Line Four

May 27, 2014

How like a prison is my cubicle
And yet how far my mind can freely roam
From gaol to Jerusalem, Hell to home.
Freedom ends or starts with a funeral.

Line four comes to us courtesy of Frank Bidart, who prescribes a period to end the preceding line. "Freedom ends or starts with a funeral" is authoritative, aphoristic, an enigma suspended between the alliterative first and last words. The line links up logically with what precedes it while introducing two major themes, "freedom" and "funeral," for us to play with in subsequent lines and stanzas.

The silver medal goes to Hazel Nolan. I liked the noble simplicity of her entry, "I take my morning constitutional," which extends the sense of "roaming" but suggests that escape is itself part of a routine. Matt Brogan ("Repair. And then, on cue, your voice: Bacall") and Pia Aliperti ("A warden knows which routes are cyclical") found ingenious rhymes. Other strong entries were Beth Gylys's string of adjectives ("Disturbed, profound, meaty, metrical"), Stacy Nott's balancing act ("With halting tread or meter musical"), and Lewis Saul's jubilation ("My imagined freedom so beautiful!"). I am happy to note that Mr. Anderson's class of smart high school seniors, victorious in line three, continues to be actively engaged. "Permanent pilgrim, canny criminal," a sweet example of double alliteration, would get votes if we opted for an adjectival rather than a declarative fourth line.

As you sharpen your pencils in pursuit of the next line, please keep in mind that the fifth line will form the first line of stanza two and must terminate in a word that we will need to rhyme, preferably in line eight, possibly earlier. The first stanza has introduced and developed the conceit of mental liberty within, or despite, physical confinement. Where do we take it, and how do we integrate it with the concept of freedom and the fact of a funeral? Or is it time to say something more about the "I" behind all these words and his or her circumstances?

Help Us Write a Sonnet: Line Five

June 3, 2014

How like a prison is my cubicle
And yet how far my mind can freely roam
From gaol to Jerusalem, Hell to home.
Freedom ends or starts with a funeral.
Say what must die inside that I may not

The fifth line of our poem in progress comes from "MQ": "Say what must die inside that I may not," a line that sustains the funereal motif in the previous line, introduces a fruitful dichotomy between "inside" and out, rhymes internally ("say what" and "may not"), and ends with a clause that may be either transitive or intransitive—you may insert a period after "not" or extend the thought into the next line. All this in perfect iambic pentameter, a quality also found in runner-up Joe Lawlor's "How deeply mourned, I wonder, would I be." Lawlor's line has further virtues: it echoes the poem's opening and leads us to a conditional while leaving its terms blank.

Third place honors are shared by Beth Gylys's "So why not indulge in the Bacchanal?" and Jonathan Galassi's "And then it's suddenly a madrigal." I like both and hope they will be resubmitted for future use. The same rhyming principle seemed at work in a line produced by a ninth-grade honors class taught by Sarah Downey: "Am I content, or am I miserable?"

I would like to thank Lloyd Schwartz, who voiced the view that our sonnet conforms to Petrarchan principles and that therefore Hazel Nolan's "I take my morning constitutional" would fit here. Equal thanks go to her for disputing that view, producing alternative lines, and characterizing our efforts to date as "very poemy," very poetical. We could use a shot of "levity" or "concreteness." It's a good point, and it helps explain my attraction to Lewis Saul's candidate for line five: "Yours, Hers, His, Mine? Cue Mozart's Requiem." From a self-described "Guest," this came in: "It's skirt suits, pant suits, pumps, bare legs or hose"—a wonderful line, but again I had the feeling that this was not the ideal place for it.

Where does that leave us? We are in poetical precincts, and sooner or later we will have to heed the imperative to leave our cloud, lower the tone, admit some levity, and add some specificity of locale and identity. But perhaps that time has not yet come. In any case, the "not" that hangs invitingly at the edge of space should act as a stimulant to the imagination. What part of the individual must vanish, be forfeited or sacrificed, for the self to endure? Has the thought come to a full stop, or will the next line ambush us? One question can be postponed. Will we have a stanza break—a line space—before line five? Possibly, even probably, but there's no need to make such specifications until we have gone further along.

A final word in defense of any formal or metrical liberties we may take. Exemplary works by such poets as Ted Berrigan and Bernadette Mayer call themselves sonnets and deserve the distinction even if the only sonnet convention they consistently observe is that the poem consists of fourteen lines. What we are writing is, by these standards, traditional and very literary, but will in the end, I feel certain, prove itself experimental, and not only because the method of composition is unusual if not unprecedented.

Help Us Write a Sonnet: Line Six

June 10, 2014

How like a prison is my cubicle,
And yet how far my mind can freely roam
From gaol to Jerusalem, Hell to home.
Freedom ends or starts with a funeral.
Say what must die inside that I may not
Cast down this die and cross the Rubicon

Line six, Anna E. Moss's "Cast down this die and cross the Rubicon," won me over with its repetition of the previous line's "die" but in a completely different sense: not the verb of mortality but a noun, the singular of dice. The line makes a cunning allusion to Julius Caesar, who said *"alea iacta est"*—"the die is cast"—when he and his armies successfully crossed the Rubicon River south of Ravenna in 49 BC.

For the second straight week, Joe Lawlor is top runner-up. He proposed a period after line five and then, "Say what must not that I may bear to live." Third place goes to Lewis Saul for sheer creativity: "Croak in Benghazi. Wasn't that your wish?" I was also taken with several smart candidates suggested by Hazel Nolan, including "Betray the grass-stained girl I used to be" and "Betray the barefoot boy, who once ran free," though I wondered whether these gender-specific constructions might prove a burden to contestants of the opposite sex.

For line seven, we have the opportunity to revitalize a trite expression ("cross the Rubicon" meaning something like "no turning back") by grounding it in fact or conjecture. What happened there in 49 BC? What does the river look like? I can imagine a continuation of the ironic comparison of the speaker with world conqueror Julius Caesar. But it is not my poem—it is ours, and I depend on your ingenuity, ladies and gentlemen. Oh, and we need to rhyme the next line, if only loosely, with "Rubicon." A tall order? No taller than "cubicle," with which it shares the same foundational consonants. "Leprechaun," "marathon," and "Novocaine" would be equally eligible, to give some examples that come to mind.

Help Us Write a Sonnet: Line Seven

June 17, 2014

How like a prison is my cubicle,
And yet how far my mind can freely roam
From gaol to Jerusalem, Hell to home.
Freedom ends or starts with a funeral.
Say what must die inside that I may not
Cast down this die and cross the Rubicon
Thence to the true hell: the heat of Tucson

In the competition for line seven, Lewis Saul's "Thence to the true hell: the heat in Tucson" prevailed in the end because it swiftly conducts us from ancient Rome to contemporary Arizona by way of the allegorical landscape of the inferno introduced in line three.

Jerry Williams ("Or beat a fake retreat like Genghis Khan") and Paul Michelsen ("With luck I'll bang a gong with Genghis Khan") made me smile, and I was tempted by Millicent Caliban's brilliant rhyme and promise of office romance: "Seduce the boss and try this ruby on." A popular song lurked behind Jamie's musical "For I will carry on, my wayward son." Christa Whitsett Overbeck boldly offered a total change of direction: "Alter course! Submit to insurrection."

Line eight bears a big responsibility. It needs to rhyme with line five ("Say what must die inside that I may not") and to complete the first movement of the poem, for in the traditional sonnet a pivot or turn occurs after line eight.

I ask all players to limit yourselves to a maximum of five entries per week—your best five lines.

And do keep in mind the entire seven lines of our poem in progress, and not just line seven, as you vie to create our next line, please. Here is where we are so far:

How like a prison is my cubicle,   *DL*
And yet how far my mind can freely roam   *Leo Braudy*
From gaol to Jerusalem, Hell to home.   *Brian Anderson and his class*
Freedom ends or starts with a funeral.   *Frank Bidart*
Say what must die inside that I may not   *MQ*
Cast down this die and cross the Rubicon   *Anna E. Moss*
Thence to the true hell: the heat of Tucson   *Lewis Saul*

Help Us Write a Sonnet: Lines Eight and Nine

June 24, 2014

How like a prison is my cubicle,
And yet how far my mind can freely roam
From gaol to Jerusalem, Hell to home.
Freedom ends or starts with a funeral.
Say what must die inside that I may not
Cast down this die and cross the Rubicon
Thence to the true hell: the heat of Tucson
Where drug lords blaze loads of coke, meth, and pot.
Freedom starts, or ends, with a funeral,

Line eight was suggested by Diana Ferraro: "Where drug lords blaze loads of coke, meth, and pot." I like the way the line rubs our nose into a harsh reality. The succession of ten monosyllables and the strong alliteration of "r" and "l" sounds in the first part of the line clinch the deal. The line sounds a conclusive note to the first eight lines of our sonnet whether we take them as one block or as two four-line stanzas.

First runner-up is Sandra M. Gilbert's "Where seething freeways tangle in a knot." I admire "seething freeways" and how the flowing assonance of that phrase gets dead-ended abruptly. The line also has the virtue of conveying via concealment the words "free" and "not."

Third place goes to Beth Gylys's "Where cold comforts, and retirees move to rot," which artfully converts the familiar adjective-plus-noun phrase, "cold comforts," into a noun-plus-verb construction. Like Gylys, Robert Schultz dwells on the contrast between hot desert and air-conditioned interior: "And this icy office—and for what?"

Some clever entries help make the case for the pun as an underrated figure of speech. Jennifer Rapuzzi's "Let not saguaro be the farm I bought" and "Will I, 'too tough to die,' need Tombstone wrought?" are two examples. Jamie echoes Milton: "Better to reign in the desert than [to] rot." Jerry Williams has a metaphysical take ("Where thoughtlessness cremates what's left of thought") as does Charles Marsh, who opts for a biblical allusion ("Where Lazarus transformed my might to ought"). Millicent Caliban proffers some practical advice: "Which none withstands unless he smokes some pot."

For line nine, I propose to duplicate line four, with a flip of the verbs: "Freedom starts, or ends, in a funeral." The repetition with variation would impose some formal order and pattern on our efforts and perhaps point us in the right direction going forward.

Line ten need not rhyme, but contestants will want to start thinking of rhyme words—"original," "hospital," "Goneril"—for use down the line.

Here is where we are so far:

How like a prison is my cubicle,
And yet how far my mind can freely roam
From gaol to Jerusalem, Hell to home.
Freedom ends or starts with a funeral.
Say what must die inside that I may not
Cast down this die and cross the Rubicon
Thence to the true hell: the heat of Tucson
Where drug lords blaze loads of coke, meth, and pot.
Freedom starts, or ends, with a funeral,

Help Us Write a Sonnet: Line Ten

July 1, 2014

How like a prison is my cubicle,
And yet how far my mind can freely roam
From gaol to Jerusalem, Hell to home.
Freedom ends or starts with a funeral.
Say what must die inside that I may not
Cast down this die and cross the Rubicon
Thence to the true hell: the heat of Tucson
Where drug lords blaze loads of coke, meth, and pot.
Freedom starts, or ends, with a funeral.
I once watched men with Uzis guard the Pope

For line ten, I chose a strong iambic pentameter line that takes the poem in what seems to be an entirely new and totally unexpected direction: James the Lesser's "I once watched men with Uzis guard the Pope." I like the element of surprise, and the line gives us a strong narrative "I" and a great monosyllabic rhyme word. It also extends the implicit religious motif in our poem and accentuates the sense of threat animating lines seven and eight. If it is not clear where geographically we are standing, that could be because of the assumption, common to the collective unconscious, that in a dream as in a poem, we can find ourselves in Rome, Jerusalem, Tucson, not to mention allegorical places in a variety of historical eras.

I must admit I am attracted to the jolting juxtaposition and am reminded of the compositional techniques of the two Australian poets who concocted the life work of "Ern Malley" in a couple of afternoons in 1944. By favoring randomness, lifting lines from diverse sources, making false allusions, and (to quote the hoaxers) "deliberately perpetrating bad verse," they thought they were travestying modernism. To their surprise they created a classic.

There was a three-way tie for second place. MQ's "So waking, I get high as Paradise" would vault us heavenward via the double meaning of "high." Frank Bidart's aphoristic "The story of a soul is one part chance" mixes authority and mystery. Chana Bloch builds on the funereal theme of line nine: "When we can let the dead bury the dead."

I was tempted, too, by the splendid internal rhymes of Maureen's "A body in its natural crucible, ash to ash, inscrutable." At least four other candidates would get votes if the choice were entrusted to a committee: Beth Gylys's defiant "But I am neither free, nor doped, nor dead"; Lewis Saul's leap of musical logic, "Ergo a true decrescendo is God"; Diana Ferraro's "Fire wounds may heal, my honor return"; and Cathy Dee's attempt to transform the work into a love poem, "Darling, will I ever be free of you?"

It is possible to come to a few tentative conclusions about the creative process underlying our evolving "crowd-sourced" sonnet. It is growing organically, a line at a time, with frequent changes of movement or emphasis but with enough thematic and formal unity to imply an ultimate coherence. Energized by the possibility that we may stumble and fall, we are giving chance a chance; we are also testing the French surrealists' theory that a work of literary art can be the product of a collaboration and can have a life independent of the will of its creators. An accurately self-described "grumpy pedant" has pointed out that we are writing neither a Shakespearean nor a Petrarchan sonnet. To which I would reply that by twentieth-century standards—in which unrhymed sonnets became a popular form—we observe a number of conventions in rhyme and meter that set us apart from much of the free verse in the literary journals of our time.

I have few preconceptions of what line eleven will look like and own up to anticipatory excitement; I have come to count on the adventurousness and skill of our co-creators. Please feel free to punctuate the end of line ten as you will—with a comma, a period, a dash or colon or semicolon, or nothing at all.

In my mind the sonnet has begun to divide itself into two four-line stanzas followed by two consisting of three lines each. But that's subject to revision.

Here is our sonnet so far:

How like a prison is my cubicle,
And yet how far my mind can freely roam
From gaol to Jerusalem, Hell to home.
Freedom ends or starts with a funeral.
Say what must die inside that I may not
Cast down this die and cross the Rubicon
Thence to the true hell: the heat of Tucson
Where drug lords blaze loads of coke, meth, and pot.
Freedom starts, or ends, with a funeral.
I once watched men with Uzis guard the Pope

Help Us Write a Sonnet: Line Eleven

July 8, 2014

How like a prison is my cubicle,
And yet how far my mind can freely roam
From gaol to Jerusalem, Hell to home.
Freedom ends or starts with a funeral.
Say what must die inside that I may not
Cast down this die and cross the Rubicon
Thence to the true hell: the heat of Tucson
Where drug lords blaze loads of coke, meth, and pot.
Freedom starts, or ends, with a funeral.
I once watched men with Uzis guard the Pope
No hope, no hope, no hope, no hope, no hope.

Sometimes strategic repetition wins the day. Jamie proposes "No hope, no hope, no hope, no hope, no hope," and I buy it, hearing an echo of King Lear's anguish, in act 5, scene 3, of Shakespeare's great tragedy. This is what Lear utters when he learns of the death of Cordelia: "And my poor fool is hanged.—No, no, no life? / Why should a dog, a horse, a rat have life, / And thou no breath at all? Oh, thou'lt come no more, / Never, never, never, never, never."

Among other strong contenders for line eleven, I would single out Dorothy Rangel's "Whose outward gaze yet breached the guarded scope"—a robust pentameter line whose central word capitalizes on the homophonic "breech," the part of the rifle (or Uzi submachine gun) that permits the loading of a cartridge into the back of the gun's barrel. Rangel's line also recalls "Once more unto the breach, dear friends," from Shakespeare's *Henry V.*

MQ came up with several compelling possibilities. Two of the best were "The earth sins on its axis after all" and "The Body is the Spirit's velvet rope." Like the first of these, Joe Lawlor's "Our dread of God, our love of death is all" would, if resubmitted, get strong consideration for line twelve.

Many other lines impressed me with their ingenuity or aptness. Theresa M. DiPasquale offers a line in the form of a comment on the previous line: "The sacred and the violent—a trope!" Frank Bidart's "From angry men without Uzis or hope" hits a chord, and we can well understand and sympathize with the desire expressed by Debra L.: "And longed to place flowers in their barrels."

In line twelve, we are looking to complete the third quatrain of the sonnet, setting up a closing couplet. Although "funeral" may not be the easiest word in the world to rhyme with, the options range from "Goneril" or "guttural" all the way to half rhymes or part rhymes on the order of "hospital," "manual," "aerial," and "musical."

The sonnet so far:

How like a prison is my cubicle,
And yet how far my mind can freely roam
From gaol to Jerusalem, Hell to home.
Freedom ends or starts with a funeral.
Say what must die inside that I may not
Cast down this die and cross the Rubicon
Thence to the true hell: the heat of Tucson
Where drug lords blaze loads of coke, meth, and pot.
Freedom starts, or ends, with a funeral.
I once watched men with Uzis guard the Pope
No hope, no hope, no hope, no hope, no hope.

Help Us Write a Sonnet: Line Twelve

July 15, 2014

How like a prison is my cubicle,
And yet how far my mind can freely roam
From gaol to Jerusalem, Hell to home.
Freedom ends or starts with a funeral.
Say what must die inside that I may not
Cast down this die and cross the Rubicon,
Thence to the true hell: the heat of Tucson
Where drug lords blaze loads of coke, meth, and pot.
Freedom starts, or ends, with a funeral.
I once watched men with Uzis guard the Pope:
No hope, no hope, no hope, no hope, no hope.
What buzz can cheer this gloomy canticle?

It is Bastille Day as I write and reflect on our efforts to master the paradox of freedom in imprisonment—the key to the sonnet's prison-door lock.

Line twelve is provided by Sandra M. Gilbert: "What buzz can cheer this gloomy canticle?" It ends the third quatrain with a question, perfectly setting up our concluding couplet. The choice of "buzz" is inspired. Utterly contemporary, the word can refer to a state of intoxication, to noise, to the chatter of the chattering classes, and in each of these senses it fits our lines. It may be argued that the balance between "cheer" and "gloom" in our poem has tilted to the latter, but our "canticle" (if we are capable) is correctible—with the right pithy closing couplet.

Runner-up honors go to Katie Whitney for her assertive hexameter: "The wide world webbed, a pharmakon for all." The alliteration in the first half of the line is countered by the clever and erudite use of "pharmakon" in the second half. Unless they are familiar with the writings of Jacques Derrida, most readers will need to look up this strange but beguiling term from the Greek, which has two contradictory meanings: it can denote either a poison or its antidote. The philosophical ramifications of the term are so fascinating, and so beautifully applicable here, as to beat down arguments against "deliberate obscurantism"—a charge that sooner or later gets leveled at an avant-garde experiment like ours. But I like looking things up.

As a sucker for ingenious punmanship, I admired MQ's "Like every online Job, I'm terminal," where Job is either a biblical character or a way of making a living, depending on whether the J is capitalized—and where "terminal" means either "end" or "computer station."

Honorable mention goes to Joe Lawlor's "Our dread of God, our love of death is all," which was submitted before and remains a strong temptation. The end words in many of the submissions impressed me especially: Joy Jacobson's "I craft my poems, indecipherable" and "though it's a dry heat, it's still insufferable"; Paul Michelsen's "Unless one is in the inner circle"; Diana's "Capital death, a Roman numeral"; Lewis Saul's "Yet Caesar's skanky whores seem so real"; Beth Gylys's "I seek escape, the dreamer's arsenal."

Line twelve is the first in the poem to end decisively on a question mark (though we have had implicit questions concealed in previous statements), and line thirteen must begin to answer it—and to set up the last and arguably most important line of all. Iambic pentameter, if you please, and let's end the line on a strong rhyme word.

Here is our progress so far:

How like a prison is my cubicle,
And yet how far my mind can freely roam
From gaol to Jerusalem, Hell to home.
Freedom ends or starts with a funeral.
Say what must die inside that I may not
Cast down this die and cross the Rubicon,
Thence to the true hell: the heat of Tucson
Where drug lords blaze loads of coke, meth, and pot.
Freedom starts, or ends, with a funeral.
I once watched men with Uzis guard the Pope:
No hope, no hope, no hope, no hope, no hope.
What buzz can cheer this gloomy canticle?

Help Us Write a Sonnet: Line Thirteen

July 22, 2014

How like a prison is my cubicle,
And yet how far my mind can freely roam:
From gaol to Jerusalem, Hell to home.
Freedom ends or starts with a funeral.

Say what must die inside that I may not
Cast down this die and cross the Rubicon,
Thence to the true hell: the heat in Tucson,
Where drug lords blaze loads of coke, meth, and pot.

Freedom starts or ends with a funeral.
I once watched men with Uzis guard the Pope.
No hope, no hope, no hope, no hope, no hope.

What buzz can cheer this gloomy canticle?
Redemption is a swift revolving door

Go with your gut, we're told, and though the Platonic ideal of our crowd-sourced sonnet would distribute the lines in an utterly democratic fashion—each line written by a different individual, half of them men and half of them women—my gut tells me to go with repeat contributor MQ for line thirteen: "Redemption is a swift revolving door." The line, in perfect iambic pentameter (with accents falling on the second syllable of "Redemption," "is," "swift," the second syllable of "revolving," and "door"), elegantly answers the question posed in line twelve. It is an aphorism that may be said to buzz (thanks to the alliterative music of "Redemption" and "revolving") and to cheer (the great American dream of "Redemption"). The adjective makes its contribution to the line's strength: the allegorical figure of "Redemption" moves swiftly, in keeping with the speed of our line-to-line transitions. And a "revolving door" is a refreshingly low-tech way of reminding us that we are still at work, in a big office building, where people come and go and quick change is the norm.

I was tempted by Katie Whitney's "Alerts sing out of tune from my device," loving "alerts" and knowing that "device"—so critical a word in contemporary discourse—has an honored place in the history of English rhyme. (In "Kubla Khan," Coleridge's "miracle of rare device, / A sunny pleasure-dome with caves of ice" rhymes ultimately with "Paradise.") Whitney's formulation is beautifully apt to our effort because it can be said that our lines, coming from so many different authors, "sing out of tune," perhaps because we have not yet had a chance to rehearse the choir.

Aaron Fagan takes third place with "The other side is one oblivion." The wisdom here cloaks itself in riddle: if the "other side" is "one oblivion," in what sense is the same true of the side we're standing on?

Some of our poets approached the closing couplet with a thirst for escape that we associate with Friday afternoons in the office. Dorothy Rangel suggested "O grog of dreams, O five o'clock, draw near!" Sally C. pleaded for "A text inviting me to happy hour." I like the attempt to rescue "happy hour" for poetry and am also impressed by clever ways to bring our poem up to speed, as Millicent Caliban does with "Put on thy Google glass and seek to know."

Brandon Crist proposes what might be the most purely poetical entry: "Perhaps the lure of pearl will cleave the shell." I wonder whether readers think I erred in not picking it or any of the other lines that impressed me, including a few that pun on "bars," a word that applies to prisons, songs, and saloons (e.g., MQ's "When bars of song imprison what they sing").

I thank all who submitted lines.

Note that I have taken the liberty of introducing stanza breaks. The poem reads best, I think, as two four-line stanzas followed by two triplets. Please feel free to disagree.

Beth Gylys's "Will love punch in, illusory no more?" rhymes with the chosen entry and will, I hope, be resubmitted along with many other closing lines that rhyme with "door." We couldn't ask for a stronger word to rhyme with, whether we wish, as we exit, to roar or soar.

The sonnet as of now:

How like a prison is my cubicle,
And yet how far my mind can freely roam:
From gaol to Jerusalem, Hell to home.
Freedom ends or starts with a funeral.

Say what must die inside that I may not
Cast down this die and cross the Rubicon,
Thence to the true hell: the heat in Tucson
Where drug lords blaze loads of coke, meth, and pot.

Freedom starts or ends with a funeral.
I once watched men with Uzis guard the Pope:
No hope, no hope, no hope, no hope, no hope.

What buzz can cheer this gloomy canticle?
Redemption is a swift revolving door

Help Us Write a Sonnet: Line Fourteen

July 29, 2014

How like a prison is my cubicle,
And yet how far my mind can freely roam:
From gaol to Jerusalem, Hell to home.
Freedom ends or starts with a funeral.

Say what must die inside that I may not
Cast down this die and cross the Rubicon,
Thence to the true hell: the heat in Tucson,
Where drug lords blaze loads of coke, meth, and pot.

Freedom starts or ends with a funeral.
I once watched men with Uzis guard the Pope.
No hope, no hope, no hope, no hope, no hope.

What buzz can cheer this gloomy canticle?
Redemption is a swift revolving door:
A revolution ends the inner war.

You, dear contestants, saved your best for last—or next to last, as I'll explain in a minute.

There were so many strong submissions for line fourteen that I could not help wavering and flip-flopping before choosing Katie Whitney's "A revolution ends the inner war." The word "revolution," too often and too loosely used in the 1960s, is le mot juste here, applying very specifically to the mechanism of the revolving door but also implying upheaval—whether a planned insurrection or one that comes about because of a host of factors, like the Great War that began one hundred years ago. Thus the word in this context means itself and its opposite. It is lovely to have that paradoxical double meaning of "revolution," to end on the "inner war" of our conflicted made-up self, and to have the word "end" itself figure in the sonnet's final gasp.

Frank Bidart cops second-place honors with the dramatic suggestion that we end line thirteen with a comma and conclude: "Like sex. You loved sex, but survival more." Truth is not always as beautifully put.

The bronze medal goes to Paul Michelsen, who would bring us full circle with "How like a prisoner this troubadour." "Troubadour" is one among several unexpected rhymes that surfaced for "door." Consider "minotaur," "Hiroshima, Mon Amour," Poe's "Nevermore," and oh yes, a tip of the chapeau to the publication that sponsors us: Joy Jacobson's "Don't you just love *American Scholar*?"

No fewer than five candidates merit honorable mention. Aaron Fagan wittily advocates repeating "Redemption is a swift revolving door." Lewis Saul proposes that we do a theme and variations on line eleven: "No more, no more, no more, no more, no more," which would effect a fearful kind of symmetry. Beth Gylys's romantic "Will love punch in, illusory no more?"—perhaps the most optimistic ending—was in the running until the last few furlongs, as was Berwyn Moore's nod to Yeats's "The Second Coming": "That turns and spins our offices to war," where "offices" is the crucial stroke. For sheer cleverness it would be hard to top Leo Braudy's "That finds mere caesura when life is o'er," which would raise our diction and bring us to an ending that is more of a pause than a full stop. The key word is "caesura"—the technical term for a pause in the middle of a line of verse—tucked neatly here in the middle of the line.

If you thought our sonnet was finished, think again. We need a title. Please submit titles by midnight Sunday, August 3rd. And—thank you, everybody.

Here is where we are:

How like a prison is my cubicle,
And yet how far my mind can freely roam:
From gaol to Jerusalem, Hell to home.
Freedom ends or starts with a funeral.

Say what must die inside that I may not
Cast down this die and cross the Rubicon,

Thence to the true hell: the heat in Tucson
Where drug lords blaze loads of coke, meth, and pot.

Freedom starts or ends with a funeral.
I once watched men with Uzis guard the Pope:
No hope, no hope, no hope, no hope, no hope.

What buzz can cheer this gloomy canticle?
Redemption is a swift revolving door:
A revolution ends the inner war.

Help Us Write a Sonnet: The Title

August 5, 2014

Monday

How like a prison is my cubicle,
And yet how far my mind can freely roam:
From gaol to Jerusalem, Hell to home.
Freedom ends or starts with a funeral.

Say what must die inside that I may not
Cast down this die and cross the Rubicon,
Thence to the true hell: the heat in Tucson,
Where drug lords blaze loads of coke, meth, and pot.

Freedom starts or ends with a funeral.
I once watched men with Uzis guard the Pope:
No hope, no hope, no hope, no hope, no hope.

What buzz can cheer this gloomy canticle?
Redemption is a swift revolving door:
A revolution ends the inner war.

The title that fits our sonnet best, in my judgment, is "Monday." Laura
Cronk proposed it (and it was seconded by the pseudonymous "Thor-
oughly Pizzled"). "Monday" works because the thoughts of our collective
sonneteer are informed by the back-to-work (or back-to-school) blues
folks may feel on Monday mornings. And "Monday" recurs; it happens
each week, departs, and comes back, and is thus like our revolutionary
swinging door.

Other admirable one-word titles were submitted by Berwyn Moore ("Spin" and "Discharge"), MQ ("Cubiditas"), Joy Jacobson ("Sonnet"), but I would award second-place honors to Diana Ferraro's "In and Out." The simplicity of "A Revolution" (Helen Klein Ross) or just plain "Revolution" (Jane Keats) also commends itself.

Cathy McArthur Palermo's "Riding the Number Seven Line" has its specificity going for it—it's a well-known subway line between Manhattan and Queens—and it's all the better that the phrase contains the word "line." Greg P.'s "Watch the Gap" is subtle; I'd have liked it even better in the British form, "Mind the Gap." I wasn't closed-minded about "The Crowded Mind" (Katie Whitney), in which, perhaps, the image of the overloaded brain merges with that of a crowded train. Two-word phrases displaying ingenuity or charm or sometimes both surfaced: David St. John's "Resurrection Shuffle," MQ's "Smoke Break" and "Human Recourse," Anne Payne's "Cubular Vortex." And I could add three or four others that made me smile.

Lewis Saul recommends that we change the terminal stanza break— dividing the poem into three stanzas of four lines each followed by a closing couplet. I agree; the symmetry of the new arrangement is even stronger if we end line two of stanza three with a colon.

Let's leave it for future scholars to interpret the poem. I will limit myself to saying that the poem may be read as a plea from the inmates of the Bastille yearning for a revolution. According to another allegorical reading, the poem chronicles the oscillations of a mind that swings regularly from hopelessness to the prospect (or the mirage) of redemption. Other subjects the poem addresses, directly or not, include the paradox of imaginative liberty despite physical confinement; the constraints of the work place, and the lure of escape and its costs; the sonnet form and its traditions and this example in particular.

I am proud of the work we did on "Monday." Next week we initiate a brand-new contest. Please tune in, turn on, take part.

Here is the final poem:

Monday

Laura Cronk

How like a prison is my cubicle,   *DL*
And yet how far my mind can freely roam: *Leo Braudy*

From gaol to Jerusalem, Hell to home.   *Brian Anderson and his class*
Freedom ends or starts with a funeral.   *Frank Bidart*

Say what must die inside that I may not   *MQ*
Cast down this die and cross the Rubicon,   *Anna E. Moss*
Thence to the true hell: the heat in Tucson   *Lewis Saul*
Where drug lords blaze loads of coke, meth, and pot.   *Diana Ferraro*

Freedom starts or ends with a funeral.
I once watched men with Uzis guard the Pope: *James the Lesser*
No hope, no hope, no hope, no hope, no hope.   *Jamie*

What buzz can cheer this gloomy canticle?   *Sandra M. Gilbert*
Redemption is a swift revolving door: *MQ*
A revolution ends the inner war.   *Katie Whitney*

The August Haiku

August 12, 2014

Sometimes a strict adherence to the rules is the only method that makes sense. That's the case, I submit, with the haiku—the subject of this week's "Next Line, Please" contest.

A rarity among poetic forms, the haiku is indifferent to patterns of meter and rhyme and dependent entirely on syllabic count. The rules of the three-line form are few. The first and third lines must consist of exactly five syllables each. The middle line—the sandwich line, if you like—has seven syllables. Consider Ron Padgett's instructive "Haiku":

First: five syllables
Second: seven syllables
Third: five syllables

The traditional haiku may make an evocative reference to a season. With this in mind, and on the conviction that constraints are paradoxically liberating, I would add two more rules as suitable to this august Asian form: your haiku must include the word "August," and you are not allowed to use the words "I," "me," "my," or "mine."

Any rule-observant haiku submitted by midnight Sunday, August 17, is eligible. Enthusiasts, please limit yourself to a maximum of five. Title is optional.

The haiku is more versatile than people realize. Richard Wilbur is one poet who has used the haiku stanza as a building block. See his "Thyme Flowering among the Rocks," which begins:

This, if Japanese,
Would represent grey boulders
Walloped by rough seas.

For further reading, you might take a look at Robert Hass's 1995 volume *The Essential Haiku: Versions of Bashō, Buson, and Issa* with English translations of three formidable Japanese masters.

Next week we'll have a tanka contest. What's a tanka? All I'll say now is that it begins with a haiku. You'll see.

This Week's Haiku, Next Week's Tanka

August 19, 2014

Wow. I love writing haiku and am not surprised that others find the form appealing. Still, I didn't expect to see 236 entries, some of them containing as many as five haiku, not to mention others that came in over the transom. And the quality was so high that any of twenty could take the laurels. After much hemming and hawing, I picked Paul Breslin's haiku:

August

The sickle, asleep
In its shed all year, begins
To dream of ripe grain.

Farm implements—W. C. Williams's red wheelbarrow, for instance—have a distinguished history in American poetry. I like the personification of the sickle in Breslin's "August" and the way the poem captures the fleeting instant between summer and fall. The sickle is still asleep, but day is about to break, and during this period of intense rapid eye movement, when dreams are at their most vivid, what else would the sickle dream of (and wish for) but "ripe grain"? The alliteration ("sickle, asleep," "ripe grain") and the line breaks are deft.

I always think it inadvertently humorous when a sportscaster says, after witnessing a brilliant performance on ice skates or skis, that the world-class athlete involved "came up short" and would have to "settle for silver." In that spirit, Helen Klein Ross will have to settle for silver for her "Posthumous Work," which celebrates a plausible miracle: "Tree fallen in stream, / long dead by late August, but / on a branch—blossoms." Notice how she saves the key word for last, and how the three lines function as a montage of images: first you see the tree fall, then it is "long dead," but then your eye is directed up close to a branch that defies the laws of mortality.

We have a three-way tie for third place. I admire the mystery and motion in Kushal Poddar's "In August away / now a robin now nothing / below or above." You can hear the sound of one hand clapping when I read Tony Villanti's "Suzuki san says / See the full moon of August? / Ha, there is no moon." Erica Dawson divides her haiku into three quick questions: "Remember August? / Summer's obituary? / The dried river's course?"

Honorable mention goes to Lewis Saul's homage to Japanese film directors: ("Kurosawa said / 'Friend Ozu, Where's the damned plot?' / It rains in August." Theodore Seto focuses on the month's fickleness: "Janus is two-faced, / but at least he is honest. / August hides winter." Michael C. Rush does a beautiful job anthropomorphizing the last full month of summer: "The old man squats, sighs, / shakes his shrunken head. August / is now, it seems, March." Many of us dread the prospect of summer's end, but Emily Lang sounds a hopeful note by naming a Vernon Duke song (as sung by Old Blue Eyes). "August in New York: / A welcome breeze brings hints of / Autumn in New York." Isn't the parallel structure of lines one and three nice? Marissa Despain doubles the number of song titles in this sweet haiku, which reminds us that poetry is often fictive: "April in Paris, / Moonlight in Vermont can't beat / August in New York."

So many others deserve to be commended. Elizabeth S's effort is lovely: "In dark root cellar/ August peaches juicy ripe / Fill green Mason jars." Kernan Davis has a winning pun, but what I like most in his haiku is "conversing" to describe what bluejays do: "It rains in August. / Hear the conversing bluejays. / Are they reigning now?" Maureen captures current events—a truce in one conflict, an embattled mountain in another—so subtly that her poem won't date itself: "August truces hold / Then another mountain / Ouds' strings, stretched, tighten." James the Lesser's wit is on display in a "schizy haiku" that has fun with a famous poem by Robert Frost: "Three paths diverged in / August—and I, I took the / two least traveled by." David Fettig tells a narrative in seventeen syllables: "'August,' she said. That's / why she left. Skin peeling. Fruit / rotting. Love wilting." Finally Elizabeth Benedict gives vent to the August melancholy to which so many of us are susceptible: "People nearly cry / When August days are counted / They go so damn fast."

For next week, a tanka. What's a tanka? A tanka is a haiku stanza followed by a two-line stanza consisting of seven syllables each. The great Japanese poets, such as Bashō, sometimes collaborated to create renga, or linked verse, in which one poet contributes a haiku and the next poet writes a two-line tail (and then a third poet writes a haiku linked to the tail, and so on and on).

My book of Japanese linked verse is in another city as I write, so here's an example of a renga stanza that I wrote to furnish an example:

The moon is ready to rise.
Dusk comes sooner each fall day.

I ask all contestants to write a two-line stanza that can build on Mr. Breslin's winning haiku and create something new and surprising.

Oh, I almost forgot: each week's winner—going back to the beginning of our crowd-sourced sonnet in May—will receive a complimentary copy of *The Best American Poetry 2014*.

The Tanka in Toto

August 26, 2014

In the contest for the best two-line tail to Paul Breslin's haiku, the laurels go to Barbara Shine:

The wheat bends before the wind,
rehearsing its surrender.

The highly visual first line shifts our focus from the sickle to the grain—from the man-made tool to the part of nature it means to glean. The second line delivers a double jolt: "rehearsing" introduces a theatrical metaphor, and "surrender" a military one, and somehow the combination of the two terms is more sensual than it is threatening. The lines are very musical. I would single out the brilliant double alliteration of "b" and "w" words in line one and the consonantal repetition of "nd" sounds: bends, wind, surrender.

Brittany Flaherty takes second place with "Keen to shake off the shackles / Of dust and reap once again." The opening line catches our attention with the sounds of "shake" and "shackles," and the enjambment is elegant: the pause at line's end before the "shackles" turn out to be figurative ("Of dust") but no less constraining for that. It is also lovely that Flaherty's last word, "again," rhymes with "grain," the final word of the Paul Breslin haiku that forms the first stanza of our tanka.

There's a three-way tie for third place. In Beth Gylys's entry—"Who knew the sharp instrument / so longed for its beheadings?"—the last word is a devastating surprise, affecting us all the more because of the horrific beheading of an American reporter by jihadists in Iraq last week. Aaron Fagan's entry—"The twisted farmer mirrors / The snath but rises to fell"—displays a species of metaphysical wit not only in its brilliant conclusion but in the mirror imagery. It was good for this city boy to learn that "snath" denotes the handle of a scythe. Kushal Poddar's lines—"the body of water down / the ditch, dawn dons shawls of mist"—are strongly alliterative in the Hopkins manner and altogether appealing.

Honorable mention: Evelyn C. for "Beyond sleep's shade, summer stalks / still sway, slow below warm winds" and Deborah B. Shepherd for "Under the shed a stray seed / Plays hooky and dreams of spring." This week we received a collaborative entry: Huy Don proposed the first line ("World's passed, no thresh left to hold") and Joy Jacobson the second ("Grim gleams on the iron blade").

Here is the tanka in toto, consisting of Paul Breslin's haiku and Barbara Shine's two-line ending. For consistency I have capitalized the first word of the last line:

August

The sickle, asleep
In its shed all year, begins
To dream of ripe grain.

The wheat bends before the wind,
Rehearsing its surrender.

Kudos to Mr. Breslin and Ms. Shine. I think we all won.
Next week we'll start a new competition.

To enable the inclusion of several more recent columns in this collection, we skip the five weeks (September 2–October 7) devoted to an acrostic poem spelling out the middle name of Ralph Waldo Emerson, who wrote the essay from which The American Scholar *takes its name.*

The Couplet

October 14, 2014

The couplet is the building block of major English poems by Alexander Pope ("The Rape of the Lock"), John Keats ("Endymion"), and many others. The heroic or closed couplet has the virtue of being able to stand alone, abstracted from a larger work. The writing of a couplet can therefore be an end in itself—or it can prove to be the opening unit of a longer work.

Here's an example from Alexander Pope's "Essay on Criticism":

A little learning is a dangerous thing;
Drink deep, or taste not the Pierian spring.

Or consider the conclusion of Shakespeare's sonnet 73:

This thou perceivest, which makes thy love more strong,
To love that well which thou must leave ere long.

Write a rhyming couplet in which one of the end words is "fall." The lines can be of uneven length but should mention at least one autumnal color (yellow, red, orange, or brown).

Deadline: midnight, Sunday, October 18.

The Winning Couplet Grows (into a Sonnet Ghazal)

October 21, 2014

Bruce Bond provides the winning couplet (which needed to have "fall" as a rhyme word and to mention an autumnal color):

The better the book, the longer the farewell,
the leaves in amber as their shadows fall.

Here "leaves" retains its primary sense but doubles as "pages," and the slant rhyme of "farewell" and "fall" contains the letters of "fall" twice, in correct order both times. We need three red ribbons. One is for Diana Ferraro's elegant

My austral spring belies your boreal fall;
you burn brown leaves and dismiss my call

The couplet uses creative adjectives to great advantage, "austral" implying the warmth of the southern hemisphere, "boreal" suggesting the onset of a long winter. Two capricious couplets of unusual wit and charm share second-place honors. John Tranter's makes a reference to John Ashbery's "Popeye" sestina:

Popeye chuckled and scratched his balls: on the wall
he scrawled, "Explore the mall in the reddening fall."

This is matched by Terence Winch in his mix of classic films and a crucial event in the history of Christianity:

On the yellow brick road to Damascus St. Paul took a fall
as did Bogart in To Have and Have Not upon meeting Bacall.

At least three other submissions merit honorable mention. Katie Naoum's "With a red gold fire raining down, we fall / in love. The lonely branches sprawling tall"; Leonard Kress's "We lug the red-leaf-laden tarp like pall- / Bearers to curbs for trucks to haul away our fall"; and Lawrence Epstein's "Of all sad leaves that curl and fall, / The red are those I must recall." So I had a brainstorm. If we combine these seven into one entity, we will have created a sonnet—and because each couplet repeats a word, the poem may qualify as a "sonnet ghazal," to use the term coined by the poet Mariam Zafar. This is how I imagine it:

The better the book, the longer the farewell,
the leaves in amber as their shadows fall.

With a red gold fire raining down, we fall
in love. The lonely branches sprawling tall,

We lug the red-leaf-laden tarp like pall-
bearers to curbs for trucks to haul away our fall.

Of all sad leaves that curl and fall,
the red are those I must recall.

My austral spring belies your boreal fall;
you burn brown leaves and dismiss my call.

On the yellow brick road to Damascus St. Paul took a fall,
as did Bogart in To Have and Have Not upon meeting Bacall.

Popeye chuckled and scratched his balls: on the wall
he scrawled, "Explore the mall in the reddening fall."

That gives us a fall glow of amber, yellow, gold, brown, and four shades of red.

If people think this is a good idea, please feel free to propose a title. In the absence of something more specific to these lines, I would opt for the generic "Sonnet Ghazal." In any case, tune in next Tuesday for the rules governing our next venture in crowd-sourced poetry.

The Shortest Story Ever Told

October 28, 2014

Two excellent titles were proposed for the sonnet ghazal we finished last week. Diana Ferraro, mindful that "Monday" is the title of the crowd-sourced sonnet we did in spring and summer, nominates "Saturday," shrewdly forecasting a series that will not be complete until five more days get named. But the prize goes to Aaron Fagan for "The Fall inside the Fall," which sounds like a phrase in a Frank Bidart poem. It is very apt for our effort here, in which the key word is "fall" in several senses.

Here's our prompt for next week's contest:

Ernest Hemingway—perhaps at Harry's Bar, perhaps at Luchow's—once bet a bunch of fellows he could make them cry with a short story six words long. If he won the bet each guy would have to fork over ten bucks. Hemingway's six-word story was, "For Sale: Baby shoes, never worn." He won the bet.

There has been a surge of interest in the prose poem and other "short" forms—as in Alan Ziegler's outstanding new anthology, *Short*. Getting into the spirit (exemplified by one wag as "prose poems, short shorts, or couldn't finish"), contestants are asked to write the shortest story they can produce. It should be under twenty-five words and should contain the arc of a narrative. Brevity is obviously a virtue here (in addition to being the soul of wit), but the underlying rationale for the exercise is that tight constraints are paradoxically liberating for the imagination.

Due: midnight, Saturday, November 1.

Tara's Theme

November 4, 2014

First place in our "shortest story" contest—in which competitors were asked to limit themselves to twenty-five words—goes to Tara for the following:

Ghost

Eugenia shook her head. "No excuses. Jim Crow gave me a hard time; I never stooped to white powder." It was ivory foundation.

The very name of the author, conjuring the theme of *Gone with the Wind*, is one clue, and the title is another. "Jim Crow" laws, which enforced racial segregation in the postbellum South, make it pretty plain where we are. When we get to "white powder," the ambiguities multiply: cocaine? But although "ivory foundation" could be taken in a sinister light—if, for example, encountered in the immediate afterglow of reading Joseph Conrad's "Heart of Darkness"—it most likely refers to a makeup product made by Maybelline or L'Oreal. "No excuses" may be the message of a story that at its base resembles a parody of a TV commercial. But the situation of a black woman who resists passing for white is most subtly invoked. Twenty-four words, including the title; exactly twenty-five, including the author's name. Brava, Tara.

The contestant bearing the pseudonym Someone with a Clue comes in second with "Medusa never had a mirror before." The line impresses with its sheer brevity, and it obliges the reader to get acquainted or reacquainted with this compelling figure of Greek myth.

Lisa Mecham gets the bronze medal for "The train jerks forward, windows frosted with the other children's shrieks, wails. On the platform, my mother is the only one without her back turned." There is mystery here, and pathos.

Nor would I overlook Diana Ferraro's "People's Heroin(e)," which (leaving gender aside) may be read as either a clever scoping of the last six presidential years or a bold prediction of what may well befall us starting on Election Day two years from today:

"She wanted to save her country. People believed her. She won the election. The country sank lower. People couldn't believe it. She was reelected."

MD gets honorable mention for this story broken into four lines:

"Savor reminiscing about the best years of your lives."
A message sent to my high school reunion.
Written on a napkin.
From the Oscars.

The last seven words, spaced as they are, provide a nice twist and double twist, although high school reunions as a source of pathos, nostalgia, or reflection are not as fresh as one would like.

A new contest designed to test wits and stimulate the imagination will greet readers of this column next Tuesday.

Finish What Dickinson Started

November 11, 2014

The puzzle: Finish this poem by adding either two or four lines:

Soft as the massacre of Suns
By Evening's Sabres slain

The explanation: Emily Dickinson, one of the glories of American poetry, wrote brief, enigmatic poems as short as two lines, with idiosyncratic punctuation that makes heavy use of the dash. The dash is an intermediate mark—not as final as a period, more striking than a comma—and her reliance on it gives some of her poems a snappy, telegraphic power consistent with her brevity and her determination to "tell all the truth but tell it slant." Let's take a look at a Dickinson poem. Here is 1222 in the Dickinson canon:

The Riddle we can guess
We speedily despise—
Not anything is stale so long
As Yesterday's surprise—

An easily solved riddle doesn't interest us, because we value the sustained act of solving, which requires a formidable riddle. By similar logic, an excellent tennis or chess player longs for an opponent of equal ability. But what is most compelling about the poem is the meaning created by the juxtaposition of the two halves of the rhyme, specifically the idea that yesterday's news, which went from "speedy" to "stale" overnight, is like a question we answered without much effort.

Dickinson's fragmentary style sometimes leaves us guessing. For example, here is 1066 in its entirety:

Fame's Boys and Girls, who never die
And are too seldom born—

While this can be read as a complete work, the poet Mitch Sisskind acted on the assumption that it represents the beginning of a poem that Dickinson intended to finish but never did. When *The Best American Poetry* blog ran an "Emily Starts, You Finish" contest in 2008, Sisskind added these two lines:

Their epitaphs—memorialized—
Cut in water—frozen in stone.

Let's make Dickinson's 1127 the prompt for this week's competition:

Soft as the massacre of Suns
By Evening's Sabres slain

You now have the chance to add lines—either two or four—to bring this poem to completion. What do you write? Remember that Dickinson loved dashes and capital letters, that she was mysterious, and that she valued not only speed but also surprise. Deadline: midnight, Saturday, November 15.

Of Ciphers—in the Brain

November 18, 2014

The Emily Dickinson competition awakened an enthusiastic and voluminous response—no surprise, given her deserved popularity. But what did surprise me was the high quality of the submissions. Dickinson is easy to caricature but notoriously difficult to imitate well. Kudos to the contestants who took Dickinson's fragment—"Soft as the massacre of Suns / By Evening's Sabres slain"—and went to town with it.

First prize goes to Jennifer Clarvoe for her ingenious extension of the simile. Her lines offer complexity, a satisfying sound pattern ending with two full rhymes, and the sense that she has appropriated Dickinson for her own poetic agenda, which is disclosed to us in its entirety only with the last word of her poem.

Soft as the massacre of Suns
By Evening's Sabres slain—
The sense discerns—the Sense—behind
The Hand—in letters strewn
Across a barren No-man's-land
Of Ciphers—in the brain.

Dickinson's sunset image is converted into a mental landscape of "ciphers" scrawled by a "Hand," possibly divine, across a vast wasteland.

Joshua Weiner comes in second with

Soft as the massacre of Suns
By Evening's Sabres slain,
The Soul—drops down—before Dominion
To touch Noon's Hem, again

Weiner's lines have a suitably subtle rhyme scheme and the beautiful image of "Noon's hem."

There is a two-way tie for third place between M. F. Chen,

Soft as the massacres of Suns
By Evening's Sabres slain
Sweet as Nightfall's hum
Entombs Promethean Day

and Christa Whitsett Overbeck,

Soft as the massacre of Suns
By Evening's Sabre slain
That dapper Dueler night
With Satisfaction, waxes-wanes
For now Dawn's portion plays—
That sly Star—she always Feigns

Chen's last line adds a mythic as well as moral dimension. Overbeck's "sly" verses include the pleasures of sweet alliteration ("That dapper Dueler") and the speeding-up effect of "waxes-wanes." Among other impressive entries I admired Rebecca Epstein's, which ends rather than starts with the Dickinson lines; Ken Foster's striking "sky of star-bright bones"; and Ross's shrewd use of the famous Latin phrase "Morituri te salutant." I would praise, too, Susan's beautiful phrase "Armistice of Dawn" in lines she composed on November 11, Veterans Day—formerly known as Armistice Day.

Next week a new competition commences. Join us on Tuesday, November 25, for full details.

The Last Shall Be First

November 25, 2014

We love last lines. The endings of favorite novels enter the mind and lodge there. Scott Fitzgerald's majestic conclusion of *The Great Gatsby* is a favorite: "So we beat on, boats against the current, borne back ceaselessly into the past." Hemingway concludes *The Sun Also Rises* with a bitterly ironic line of dialogue enlivened by an unusual choice of adjective: "'Yes,' I said. 'Isn't it pretty to think so?'" The terseness at the end of Virginia Woolf's *Mrs. Dalloway* is no less memorable: "For there she was."

For their full impact, the great endings depend on the narratives that precede them. But a surprising number will be seen to have a meaning and a charm even when removed from their context. This is true of several of the lines I've quoted, and others spring to mind. When Dostoevsky brings *Crime and Punishment* to its finish, he leaves the door open for subsequent developments. He dangles the possibility of his hero's redemption, then says matter-of-factly: "That might be the subject of a new story—our present story is ended." Herman Melville airs a similar sentiment but with an effect that is both eerie and menacing at the close of *The Confidence Man:* "Something further may follow from this Masquerade."

The last line of Sholem Aleichem's story "A Yom Kippur Scandal"—"Gone forever"—concludes its narrative beautifully while making this reader believe it could perform the same function admirably for a half dozen others.

Your task for next week is to write the last sentence of a nonexistent story—either a story that we can imagine or one that we would yearn to read strictly on the basis of your sentence. The winning entry may imply a specific narrative—or it may be so suggestive that readers will be inspired to supply the writing that culminates in the sentence.

It doesn't have to be long—just unforgettable.

Deadline: midnight, Sunday, November 30.

The Sense of an Ending

December 2, 2014

Many thanks to all who entered our competition for the best last sentence of a narrative that does not (or does not yet) exist. In the end, for the end, I chose Kempy Bloodgood's "And that was just the beginning." I like its crispness. It consists of only six words, of which just one is polysyllabic. The line has been used before, in one guise or another, although that should probably not prejudice us against it. Philip Roth's *Portnoy's Complaint* concludes with the doctor saying, "Now vee may perhaps to begin. Yes?"

I recall "Station Baranovich," a story by Sholem Aleichem in which a tale-teller on a train regales his traveling companions with a curious story full of twists and turns. Suddenly he realizes that the train has reached his stop, Baranovich. He grabs his bag and races for the exit. One of the listeners tries to stop him. "What happened next?" they want to know. "We won't let you go until you tell us the end." The tale-teller is now on the platform and the train is about to pull out. "What end?" he says. "It was just the beginning." The story's last line: "May Station Baranovich burn to the ground!"

Millicent Caliban's entry—"They shuddered as they heard the gates clang shut, then hand in hand, continued slowly along the way spread out before them"—also echoes a noble predecessor, in this case Milton's *Paradise Lost*: "They hand in hand with wandering steps and slow, / Through Eden took their solitary way."

Maureen has a pair of sentences that struck me as promising: "It's the last time she slipped a stitch" and "He'll always be glad for her hairpin."

And Kushal Poddar got some votes in the committee of my mind for "And we waited for him to turn his head, and we waited." The repetition of the verb vibrates eerily in the air.

Next Tuesday we shall have a new competition. If you have an idea for a good prompt, please feel free to enter it here in the comment field. You never know.

Rhyme Sandwich

December 9, 2014

Everyone who likes rhymes and jokes has at least one good limerick in him or her. No one has yet figured out a way to put the limerick to anything but lighthearted use. But the British poet Wendy Cope showed great originality in paraphrasing (and parodying) the five sections of T. S. Eliot's "The Waste Land" as five limericks.

The five lines of a limerick amount to a rhyme sandwich, an eminently suitable form for saucy wit. The best limericks are bawdy but too good-natured to seem truly obscene. Their humor keeps offense at bay.

Here's a famously anonymous example that has made it into several light-verse anthologies:

An Argentine gaucho named Bruno
Said, "Sex is one thing I do know.
Women are fine,
And sheep just divine,
But a llama is numero uno."

The limerick is an occasion to display wit and cleverness. An internal rhyme adds to the fun, as in the third and fifth lines of the following:

While Titian was mixing rose madder,
His model reclined on a ladder.
Her position to Titian
Suggested coition,
So he leapt up the ladder and had her.

On the theory that constraints liberate the imagination, I propose that your limerick contain "Mabel" and "brandy" as rhyme words.

Good luck—and remember: the more fun you have composing a limerick, the more fun your readers and listeners will have when you share it with them. Deadline: midnight, Sunday, December 13.

Hot Toddy

December 16, 2014

To this bon vivant, the limericks you wrote featured just the right amount of mixology and sexology. There was a photo finish, and the winner by a nose was Rebecca Epstein's

There once was a man named Abel
Whose thirst was insati-able.
All day he lapped brandy
That tasted like candy,
But at night his hot toddy was Mabel.

The ostentatious cleverness of the initial rhyme gets us right into the spirit of things, and the cocktail named in the final line goes down like a rum grog in a candlelit chamber.

So "Hot Toddy," as I think of it, gets the win, while this unheralded entry from someone named "Someone with a Clue" finished strong and took second place:

"I'll give you a choice," said Mabel,
(Who'd screw any drunk in a label),
To the smooth-talking dandy,
With fine taste in brandy,
"On top or under the table?"

It may have the best last line. I admired, too, the way "label" in the second line works as shorthand for a certain type of fashion-conscious professional male of the species.

Of James the Lesser's several impressive entries, the one about able "Andy" finished in the money:

There once was a sweetheart named Andy,
whose 'tastes' were exceedingly randy.
Of what he was able,

ask Doris, or Mabel—
or Jessica, Alice, or Brandi.

The closure conveys a sense of mighty prowess in beautifully under-stated rhetoric. A clever feat, it reminded me of what can be done when restraint and repetition are yoked—as in the final stanzas of Edwin Arlington Robinson's "Miniver Cheevy," a poem I heartily recommend.

Reagan Upshaw deserves honorable mention for the sophistication of sensibility and vocabulary here on display:

An overindulgence in brandy
Had Chaplin the Tramp feeling randy.
He called out to Mabel
"I want you in déshabil-
Lé, with a camera handy!"

Though it didn't use the suggested rhyme scheme, Carlos Alcala's lim-erick may be the naughtiest in the old-fashioned sense, and if this were chess, where extraordinary moves get exclamation points (also known as screamers), I'd place one after the second and fifth lines, for the collo-quial excellence of the former and the reference to Thelonious Monk's piano jazz of the other.

At the abbey, the Sisters were drunk
On the sacrament, who woulda thunk?
One nun quit her habit
For an unrighteous abbot,
And played with felonious monk

If you're wondering, I chose "brandy" and "Mabel" as possible end words for two reasons. One was Ogden Nash's "Reflections on Ice-Breaking" ("Candy / Is dandy, / But liquor / Is quicker."). The second is that W. H. Auden in one of his speculative essays postulates that nearly all writers "are either Alices or Mabels." For example, according to Auden, Virginia Woolf is an Alice, while James Joyce is a Mabel. Figuring out what Auden meant by this classification, which is accompanied by two passages from Lewis Carroll, would itself make for a fine parlor game.

Next week: another contest. Please feel free to share ideas, sugges-tions, and prompts.

When Two Strangers Meet

January 6, 2015

I like keeping a notebook in which I scribble down overheard dialogue, a pun or a typo that catches my eye, lists of similes, possible opening lines for poems or stories. Sometimes I find myself lifting just a part of the opening sentence of a book—the first part. I delete the rest and with the passage of time, I can approach it as a literary problem to be creatively solved.

OK, quick: without looking it up, how would you complete a first sentence that begins "In my younger and more vulnerable years, my father gave me . . ." You may not outdo the author of *The Great Gatsby*, but it's worth trying.

Leaving *Gatsby* aside, I suggest we try this experiment. Here are the first twenty words of a piece of writing—whether a story, a prose poem, or a novella:

On the Sunday after Christmas, in a nondescript cocktail lounge at a forlorn Midwestern airport, two stranded passengers met and . . .

Finish the paragraph, adding as many as fifty words. Deadline: midnight, January 11.

Airport Buoyancy

January 13, 2015

Among the many excellent entries this week, a strong element of surprise is what distinguished the two best pieces. I would divide this week's prize between Rachel Barenblat and Nin Andrews—or maybe I should say I will double the prize, as each of them will receive a complimentary copy of *The Best American Poetry 2014*.

Barenblat laces her prose with poetry, a poetic diction festooned with hyperbole, with flower petals and blank verse, for the purposes of satirical exaggeration. She captures the intoxication of a chance encounter with a stranger: there is buoyancy because there are no responsibilities and, alas, no future. I love how her piece functions as a critique of the poetical, with "business cards and Twitter handles" bringing us back to earth. Here's her entry:

On the Sunday after Christmas, in a nondescript cocktail lounge at a forlorn Midwestern airport, two stranded passengers met and the planet tilted off its axis. Birds flew down from the rafters and offered serenades. Customer service representatives began speaking in blank verse. Children scattered flower petals. Glitter rained down from the ceilings. The passengers exchanged business cards and Twitter handles. Their steps released the scent of roses as they boarded their separate planes.

Andrews introduces the complexity of a human encounter between a self-described "bimbo" in lace stockings, black pumps, and red fingernails, and the man she has agreed to have a drink with: "I know what you are," he says—and the writer leaves it unclear whether he speaks smugly, with menace, and toward what goal. But what charms this reader most is the implication that the bimbo act may be deliberate and is something worthy of attention, perhaps with Erving Goffman's *The Presentation of Self in Everyday Life* on our side. This is what Nin wrote:

On the Sunday after Christmas, in a nondescript cocktail lounge at a forlorn Midwestern airport, two stranded passengers met and ordered drinks. The woman, wearing a powder-blue dress, lace stockings, and black pumps waved her red fingernails in the air and fluttered nervously like a rare African bird. She was playing the part of a bimbo well, she thought, before the man leaned forward and whispered, I know what you are.

The runner-up is Marlon Howell who scores with speed—the rapidity with which he reaches the plot twist. His description of a chance encounter between strangers on the way to the same funeral can stand on its own as a prose poem and should be published as such. The "two cheap bourbons" is a nice touch. I encourage him to come up with a good title for this two-sentence parable:

On the Sunday after Christmas, in a nondescript cocktail lounge at a forlorn Midwestern airport, two stranded passengers met and, while exchanging banalities and bemoaning the poor weather, learned that both were traveling to attend funerals. An hour and two cheap bourbons later they discovered that it was the same funeral.

Honorable mention: Frank Tomasulo's Pinteresque dialogue, Maureen's robotic future, Brian Tholl's tattoos, and Alan Ziegler's oenophilia.

My thanks to all who took part. As ever, I appreciate the creative effort.

Let's Write a Sestina

January 20, 2015

The sestina, a verse form dating back to the Middle Ages, consists of thirty-nine lines divided into seven stanzas: six containing six lines each and a concluding triplet. With its intricate rules, the form may seem hugely intimidating at first. In fact, however, the sestina has enjoyed great popularity among modern poets. You'll find six examples of the form in *The Oxford Book of American Poetry*: two by Elizabeth Bishop, one each from Ezra Pound, Anthony Hecht, Harry Mathews, and James Cummins, and only lack of space prevented the inclusion of a seventh, John Ashbery's "The Painter."

The same six words end all thirty-nine lines in a sestina. These end words (known in the trade as "teleutons") must appear in a predetermined order. If the teleutons of stanza one are designated by the numbers one, two, three, four, five, and six, in the next stanza the same words must appear in this order: six, one, five, two, four, three. The same 6–1–5–2–4–3 pattern continues until we reach the end of the sixth stanza at which point the end words line up in their original order. In the seventh stanza—ah, but that can wait.

We will write our crowd-sourced sestina in seven sessions, one stanza a week. For week one, your job is simply to write an opening stanza, using the following end words in any order:

Port
Fear
Spirit
Dress
Book
Sing

You are entitled to take liberties. The word "port" can refer to a harbor or a kind of wine—or you can resort to variants such as "report," "airport," "support," "sport." You may use "fear" as either a verb or a noun. The same with "dress" and even "book." Worry less about what you're saying than about writing arresting lines that fit the pattern. Have fun; surprise yourself.

A paradox of the form is that although it looks daunting, in practice it can liberate the imagination. You're so busy trying to solve a puzzle that you don't get in the way of the poem emerging like a straight shot from your deep consciousness. John Ashbery has likened the writing of a sestina to "riding a bicycle downhill and letting the pedals push your feet." Just how apt that simile is we'll soon see, I promise.

Please post your entries by the deadline, midnight, Saturday January 24.

Winning Stanza Refuses to Cave

January 27, 2015

My compliments. Virtually every entry had something going for it, and I loved the enthusiastic way people threw caution to the wind in playing with the sestina form.

For best opening stanza I choose this by Diane Seuss for the coherence of the narrative and the spectacular reiteration of "cave" as a synonym for "capitulate":

Finally the veins give out and they stick in a port
for the blood draws. Veins cave before the spirit.
Spirit caves before the voice stops the sing-song
of moan and groan that tolls all night like a book
of hymns without words. After a while even fear
caves, like a dress without a body or an address.

Diane Seuss has given us a setting and situation (medical), with an air of resignation that gets abruptly corrected when "even fear / caves, like a dress without a body." That is a lovely simile and a brilliant turn for the stanza to take.

There's a four-way tie for second place: the honors get divvied among LaWanda Walters, Patricia Smith, Angela Ball, and Spider Milkshake. (Their stanzas appear below.)

OK, our next six-line stanza must end in this pattern:

dress (as a word or a suffix)
port
fear
spirit
book
song (or sing)

Note that the 6-1-5-2-4-3 progression ensures that the last word in each stanza will be identical with the word ending the first line of the next stanza. This generates a certain amount of continuity and momentum. It underscores, too, that repetition, far from being a fault, is a key musical element in poetry.

The trick will be how to use the material Diane gave us and to amalgamate something new to the mix. One tip: try sneaking in the word "cave" whether in the verb or noun sense.

Deadline: midnight, January 26, 2015.

The texts of the runners-up:

After dessert, the men retire to take their port
and cigars in the library, the women sing
and play the Brodmann piano. But their spirits
are low, there is something they all fear.
A moonstone, a woman in a white dress—
there are hints of things to come in books.

LaWanda Walters

Sestina's stuffy form I fear
a challenge to poetic spirit.
Examples from the Oxford book—
though their praises I might sing—
my words n'er shall sestina dress
without assist from tawny port.

Patricia Smith

Peaks have yellow flowers for their dress.
At the verge of a torn-off road, spirits
waive the right of way. Rene Magritte's book
says, "Painting makes poetry visible." His port
is the one that opens the storm. "Fear
sees what is hidden, finds a throat, sings."

Angela Ball

Our wonderment is the sun on our tribal dress,
winding through our skull as wind in the pages of a book
designed to part the waves in our spirit
and deliver us to safe port.
Does it wonder us to find these pages sing
yet lie, promising comfort, delivering fear?

Spider Milkshake

Chemosabe

February 3, 2015

I couldn't be more delighted with the entries we are getting for our crowd-sourced sestina. For our second stanza, I opt for Angela Ball's:

> For life off-trend, beyond fashion, Mary K. wore no day dress,
> only "gowns." She larked about chemo: "Any port
> in a storm." When the doctor said, "Bad news," fear
> was a vanity she dismissed: "Anodynes will keep my spirits
> lit." She read scripture, began a memoir, a prose-poem book—
> "not illness stuff"—but original woods, night-born foals, evensong.

Angela's stanza sustains the medical metaphor introduced in stanza one—"chemo," "port," "doctor," "illness"—and complicates it in fascinating ways, literary ("a memoir, a prose-poem book") as well as religious ("scripture," "evensong"). The tone is unusual—"she larked"—and there seem to be many possible directions for our next stanza, where the end words must appear in this order:

song
dress
book
port
spirit
fear

Second place: Patricia Smith.
Third place: Rachel Barenblat.
Honorable mention: James the Lesser (the stanza beginning "Trembling . . . I look up your dress, your address") and Charise Hoge. These worthy stanzas (as well as those of Smith and Barenblat) will be found in the "Comments" section of last week's post ("Winning Stanza Refuses to Cave") on *The American Scholar* website.

It pleases me to see the cross-exchanges among us, which have the salutary effect of making us realize that we are collaborators as much as competitors.

Here's our poem in full at this point:

Finally the veins give out and they stick in a port
for the blood draws. Veins cave before the spirit.
Spirit caves before the voice stops the sing-song
of moan and groan that tolls all night like a book
of hymns without words. After a while even fear
caves, like a dress without a body or an address.

For life off-trend, beyond fashion, Mary K. wore no day dress,
only "gowns." She larked about chemo: "Any port
in a storm." When the doctor said, "Bad news," fear
was a vanity she dismissed: "Anodynes will keep my spirits
lit." She read scripture, began a memoir, a prose-poem book—
"not illness stuff"—but original woods, night-born foals, evensong.

Deadline: midnight, Saturday, February 6.

"Her Winsome Style"

February 10, 2015

Something wonderful is happening with our crowd-sourced sestina. The people crafting their stanzas have formed a community, appreciative of one another's efforts, with the effect that we are really collaborating as much as competing—which is a great victory for aesthetics and for sportsmanship in a realm (poetry) where fangs often come out.

My choice for this week's winning stanza was not an easy one, but after hemming and hawing I went with this by Charise Hoge:

Visitors spark with lyrics of ballads, of songs,
a lamentation for the lack of redress
to tip the scale of slippery life. She jests, "Book
me a room with a courtyard and easy transport."
A smile dawns on her lips this cup won't pass; her spirit
a salve on tarnished will, her winsome style to balk at fear.

For the second straight week, Patricia Smith takes second prize:

Accept ambition's wane. Summon matins, evensong.
Perhaps avoid the gown today in favor of the dress?
No need to rush, it takes a while—to write that book:
gather thoughts of other times, adventures due report,
rousing fresh ideas that will lift the spirit
up. Ah, perfect antiseptic to cleanse the port of fear.

Of several worthy efforts by Paul Michelsen, I choose this for third place:

Funeral plans roughly mapped out, songs
to be sung at services, the final dress.

Last Will and Testament signed, re-reading the "wish" book.
Myriad ways of seeing the phrase "on life support".
Touch head (Father), chest (Son), shoulder (Holy), shoulder (Spirit).
Heard once the Good Book says 365 times not to fear.

Honorable (and grateful) mention goes to Angela Ball and LaWanda Walters.

So this is what our sestina looks like at this point:

Finally the veins give out and they stick in a port
for the blood draws. Veins cave before the spirit.
Spirit caves before the voice stops the sing-song
of moan and groan that tolls all night like a book
of hymns without words. After a while even fear
caves, like a dress without a body or an address.

For life off-trend, beyond fashion, Mary K. wore no day dress,
only "gowns." She larked about chemo: "Any port
in a storm." When the doctor said, "Bad news," fear
was a vanity she dismissed: "Anodynes will keep my spirits
lit." She read scripture, began a memoir, a prose-poem book—
"not illness stuff"—but original woods, night-born foals, evensong.

Visitors spark with lyrics of ballads, of songs,
a lamentation for the lack of redress
to tip the scale of slippery life. She jests, "Book
me a room with a courtyard and easy transport."
A smile dawns on her lips this cup won't pass; her spirit
a salve on tarnished will, her winsome style to balk at fear.

In the next stanza, the end words must appear in this order:

fear
song
spirit
dress

port
book

I have no doubt that by the time we finish our work, each of our dedicated participants will have contributed at least one stanza to the mix.

Deadline: Saturday, February 14, midnight any time zone.

Sestina: Stanza Four

February 17, 2015

I cannot remember a poetry contest in which (1) the entries were so consistently high, (2) the competitors were avid collaborators, (3) the exchanges among contestants were so lively and heartfelt, and (4) the excitement felt by all was so palpable. Kudos all around.

Of nine finalists, each of which has its notable virtues, I picked James the Lesser's stanza, which begins with bold aphorisms, segues to our protagonist, makes a metaphysical distinction ("she separated spirit / from Spirit"), opts for comic relief ("the Colbert Report"), and concludes with a triple iteration of the word "book," whether biblical or secular. The stanza continues our main line while opening new possibilities for stanza five. Here's what James the Lesser proposes:

To speak of bravery is to speak of fear.
To lose oneself in singing is not to hear the song.
Awake in the night-dark, damp, she separated spirit
from Spirit, considered sightlines of corpse-dress.
Sometimes she laughed till tears came at the Colbert Report:
the good book is a good book, yes, but just a book.

Second place goes to Thelmadonna for her splendid portrait of our heroine, Mary:

Even as a child Mary scoffed at fear,
her own or anyone's. Citing some brave girl from book or song
she swam the flood-filled ditch, trespassed old houses, said her holy spirit
thrived on chance and mystery, like Nancy Drew's. Undress
her now, you'd see the ancient scars, the port-
wine birthmark on her breast, her famous tat: This body for a book.

Third place is taken by Christine Rhein for a rather different if complementary profile of our protagonist—in this case "Mary Marvel" by name:

Hard work, of course—pretending to be fearless,
tuning out the thrum inside her, that off-key song.
When the doctors, nurses praise her "fighting spirit,"
she thinks of childhood, bullies, her flowered dresses.
What harm in picturing a lightning bolt atop the port,
herself as Mary Marvel, the memoir turned to comic book?

Honorable mention: Paul Michelsen, Charise Hoge, Angela Ball, Rachel Barenblat, Patricia Smith, LaWanda Walters.

I am almost tempted to choose *all* of their stanzas and go on to multiply the number of sestinas that we produce—in the manner of the French author Raymond Queneau, who created a hundred thousand billion sonnets (that is, ten to the fourteenth power) simply by writing ten sonnets with the exact same rhyme scheme and interchangeable lines.

Here is our extraordinary sestina so far:

Finally the veins give out and they stick in a port
for the blood draws. Veins cave before the spirit.
Spirit caves before the voice stops the sing-song
of moan and groan that tolls all night like a book
of hymns without words. After a while even fear
caves, like a dress without a body or an address.

For life off-trend, beyond fashion, Mary K. wore no day dress,
only "gowns." She larked about chemo: "Any port
in a storm." When the doctor said, "Bad news," fear
was a vanity she dismissed: "Anodynes will keep my spirits
lit." She read scripture, began a memoir, a prose-poem book—
"not illness stuff"—but original woods, night-born foals, evensong.

Visitors spark with lyrics of ballads, of songs,
a lamentation for the lack of redress
to tip the scale of slippery life. She jests, "Book
me a room with a courtyard and easy transport."

A smile dawns on her lips this cup won't pass; her spirit
a salve on tarnished will, her winsome style to balk at fear.

To speak of bravery is to speak of fear.
To lose oneself in singing is not to hear the song.
Awake in the night-dark, damp, she separated spirit
from Spirit, considered sightlines of corpse-dress.
Sometimes she laughed till tears came at the Colbert Report:
the good book is a good book, yes, but just a book.

For next week, stanza five, we need the end words to occur in this order:

book
fear
port
song
dress
spirit

Midnight, Saturday, February 21, is our deadline. Good luck, everyone—
and thank you for your ingenuity, hard work, wit, and whimsy.

Stanza Five: "Six Options"

February 24, 2015

There are sestinas in which one of the six words is a variable. I have myself written such a sestina: the title poem of my book *Operation Memory* has five regular end words and one variable. The variable is a number and occurs in descending order: one hundred, fifty, eighteen, ten, 1970, one and, in the triplet closing the poem, a million. The end words themselves are meant to convey a story.

So what I am proposing to do here is not utterly unprecedented.

I propose that we have six winners for stanza five.

That will give us, when we complete our work, six sestinas—the perfect number for a verse form that relies on six end words.

True, we will have created a dilemma for ourselves when we complete stanza six and the three-line envoy and decide upon a title. Which stanza five shall we choose? Of the six sestinas, which shall we post on the site? Shall we vote—the same week that we choose a title? It is, as dilemmas go, a happy one to have—with shades of Cortázar and Queneau and other fabulous experimentalists who incorporate formal options in their writing.

I will preface a comment before each of the six candidates that I offer here as finalists that double as cowinners.

1. Rachel Barenblat: The play on "making book" is priceless, and I have a personal weakness for Chet Baker, jazz trumpeter and singer, even if the allusion is to his sad end in Amsterdam.

The odds of her survival? Mary makes book,
nudging visitors to place their bets. She doesn't fear.
The darkness around us is deep; so what? That's of no import.
She jitterbugs with her IV pole, humming the song
Chet Baker played before hurtling to his last address.
When the body gives up the ghost, what's left: just spirit.

2. Paul Michelsen: Each line in the following stanza contains an iteration of the word "just," a lovely effect.

Yes, the book that helps her to be not afraid is just a book
to those who still fear death. Just a bunch of words for those who fear
where we will and will not go. Wishing she could just teleport
herself to certain places, even just for minutes here and there. Songs
take her there kinda-sorta, but it's just not enough today. That
    transformative dress
double dog dares her from a closet far away, "Just put me on in spirit."

3. Charise Hoge: I like—the internal rhymes ("career . . . fear . . . year") and striking simile transitioning into the spiritual elevation accompanied by those high heels in the last line.

Is it just—what if she throws out the book,
starts a second career of needling fear,
designs plans for another year, deports
her foreign cells to a singular song
that lasts as long as an epitaph, dresses
in heels to reveal her elevated spirit?

4. Christine Rhein: For her development of Mary's character, so seamless you wouldn't suspect that there are six repeating words running the show:

She thinks of her laden shelves, the thick textbooks
she trudged through, the boy she didn't marry, how fear
can squander a life. Above her heart, the pumping port
is silent. Again, she's free to hum any old song.
Again: Sum-mer-time and . . . This season's dress—
hospital green. But her veil—a fuchsia spirit.

5. Angela Ball: Here we have the introduction of romance—a medical romance that blends contemporary idioms (PTSD) with recent history ("the 'Nam vet") and ends on a high spiritual note.

A therapist arrived—"I'm John, the 'Nam vet you convinced to hit the books,
achieve my dream of being a PT. Your counseling made the difference,
     calmed my fear
of the world, my PTSD. Let's see if I can help your legs feel better. The report
says you have lost mobility." Mary smiled, cried a little, felt like singing.
"It's wonderful you're here," she said. "Wish I had on something nice, a dress,
not this rumpled gown." "What for?" he asked. "What matters is your spirit."

6. James the Lesser: The continuation of the examination of the "good book" ("the good book is a good book, yes, but just a book—") commends itself, and the conception of a divinity whimsically arrived at seems to suit the complexities of our heroine's personality.

although the only thing between you and madness IS a book,
sometimes. For all the ways she thumbed her nose at fear,
some nights her lonely ship couldn't escape that port,
her "skull & crossbones" hanging limply like a sad song . . .
Until she'd laugh. She could still mix metaphors to redress
self-pity! Maybe there WAS a god, after all, tending her spirit.

There are three runners-up. Patricia Smith's stanza conducts us from poems and books, to a yoga mantra, as spirit dances in its "hospital-dress." LaWanda Walters develops Mary's character by strictly bibliographic means. J. F. McCullers's stanza has a rhythm that is hard to resist.

When you submit your candidate for stanza six, please indicate which of these stanzas (or which of several of them) your stanza follows.

Here is the order in which the end words must appear in stanza six:

spirit
book
dress
fear
song
port

Deadline: Saturday, February 21, midnight any time zone.

Here is the complete sestina so far:

Finally the veins give out and they stick in a port
for the blood draws. Veins cave before the spirit.
Spirit caves before the voice stops the sing-song
of moan and groan that tolls all night like a book
of hymns without words. After a while even fear
caves, like a dress without a body or an address.   *Diane Seuss*

For life off-trend, beyond fashion, Mary K. wore no day dress,
only "gowns." She larked about chemo: "Any port
in a storm." When the doctor said, "Bad news," fear
was a vanity she dismissed: "Anodynes will keep my spirits
lit." She read scripture, began a memoir, a prose-poem book—
"not illness stuff"—but original woods, night-born foals, evensong.   *Angela Ball*

Visitors spark with lyrics of ballads, of songs,
a lamentation for the lack of redress
to tip the scale of slippery life. She jests, "Book
me a room with a courtyard and easy transport."
A smile dawns on her lips this cup won't pass; her spirit
a salve on tarnished will, her winsome style to balk at fear.   *Charise Hoge*

To speak of bravery is to speak of fear.
To lose oneself in singing is not to hear the song.
Awake in the night-dark, damp, she separated spirit
from Spirit, considered sightlines of corpse-dress.
Sometimes she laughed till tears came at the Colbert Report:
the good book is a good book, yes, but just a book.   *James the Lesser*

Stanza Six: Mary's Tip

March 3, 2015

The entries this week were so solid that I found myself hemming, hawing, flipping, and flopping until finally and quite impulsively I chose Angela Ball's candidate for stanza six, composed (she tells us) "to follow Christine Rhein's lovely stanza."

This solves two problems, at least tentatively, as I can now summarize our efforts in a six-stanza sestina lacking only a three-line envoi and a title.

Here goes:

Finally the veins give out and they stick in a port
for the blood draws. Veins cave before the spirit.
Spirit caves before the voice stops the sing-song
of moan and groan that tolls all night like a book
of hymns without words. After a while even fear
caves, like a dress without a body or an address.　　　　*Diane Seuss*

For life off-trend, beyond fashion, Mary K. wore no day dress,
only "gowns." She larked about chemo: "Any port
in a storm." When the doctor said, "Bad news," fear
was a vanity she dismissed: "Anodynes will keep my spirits
lit." She read scripture, began a memoir, a prose-poem book—
"not illness stuff"—but original woods, night-born foals, evensong.　　　　*Angela Ball*

Visitors spark with lyrics of ballads, of songs,
a lamentation for the lack of redress
to tip the scale of slippery life. She jests, "Book
me a room with a courtyard and easy transport."
A smile dawns on her lips this cup won't pass; her spirit
a salve on tarnished will, her winsome style to balk at fear.　　　　*Charise Hoge*

To speak of bravery is to speak of fear.
To lose oneself in singing is not to hear the song.
Awake in the night-dark, damp, she separated spirit
from Spirit, considered sightlines of corpse-dress.
Sometimes she laughed till tears came at the Colbert Report:
the good book is a good book, yes, but just a book.

                                                                    James the Lesser

She thinks of her laden shelves, the thick textbooks
she trudged through, the boy she didn't marry, how fear
can squander a life. Above her heart, the pumping port
is silent. Again, she's free to hum any old song.
Again: Sum-mer-time and . . . This season's dress—
hospital green. But her veil—a fuchsia spirit.

                                                                    Christine Rhein

Mary's tip: Don't say we died "fighting a courageous battle," spirit
unbowed. Don't sport pins signaling "awareness," don't book
tickets for charity-auction-banquet noblesse oblige. Don't dress
incredulous linebackers in pink cleats; claim envy for our fear-
lessness, admiration for our grace; de-compose us in a drippy song
of Spirit's brave skiff aimed shoreward. A slab is no damn port.

                                                                    Angela Ball

    The beauty of the sestina form is that after six times around the track, the initial order of the end words is restored, only we must place them within three lines. Line one should ideally have "port" in the middle and "spirit" at the end; line two should have "song" in the middle and "book" at the end; and line three should have "fear" in the middle and "dress" at the end. There are no sestina police, and a lot of leeway, so let's not get too hung up on details.

    I continue to regard what we have done here as a collaboration more than a contest—an act of community. We have created a character, a crisis, and a coherent narrative: something quite remarkable, from the first word on.

    The exchanges among the poets taking part remain one of the highlights of this project.

    Let's have your candidates for the poem's conclusion by Saturday, March 6, midnight any time zone.

Envoi: Melodious Song

March 10, 2015

The candidates for our sestina's envoi are as good as I could have hoped. I sat on the fence between Patricia Smith's smart use of interruption and ellipsis:

Was she adrift . . . her port . . . somehow spirited
away? Melodious song . . . number 342, maroon book . . .
"Be not afraid" . . . banish fear . . . select a dress . . .

and Christine Rhein's affirmative "hallelujah":

But when the nurses smile—the port removed—her spirit
once more sings—Hallelujah!—her body, a battered book,
taped anew, no fear showing. For now, her wounds all dressed.

    A great case could be made for either, but in the end I went for the former, and here is our sestina:

Finally the veins give out and they stick in a port
for the blood draws. Veins cave before the spirit.
Spirit caves before the voice stops the sing-song
of moan and groan that tolls all night like a book
of hymns without words. After a while even fear
caves, like a dress without a body or an address.

Diane Seuss

For life off-trend, beyond fashion, Mary K. wore no day dress,
only "gowns." She larked about chemo: "Any port
in a storm." When the doctor said, "Bad news," fear
was a vanity she dismissed: "Anodynes will keep my spirits

lit." She read scripture, began a memoir, a prose-poem book—
"not illness stuff"—but original woods, night-born foals, evensong.   *Angela Ball*

Visitors spark with lyrics of ballads, of songs,
a lamentation for the lack of redress
to tip the scale of slippery life. She jests, "Book
me a room with a courtyard and easy transport."
A smile dawns on her lips this cup won't pass; her spirit
a salve on tarnished will, her winsome style to balk at fear.   *Charise Hoge*

To speak of bravery is to speak of fear.
To lose oneself in singing is not to hear the song.
Awake in the night-dark, damp, she separated spirit
from Spirit, considered sightlines of corpse-dress.
Sometimes she laughed till tears came at the Colbert Report:
the good book is a good book, yes, but just a book.   *James the Lesser*

She thinks of her laden shelves, the thick textbooks
she trudged through, the boy she didn't marry, how fear
can squander a life. Above her heart, the pumping port
is silent. Again, she's free to hum any old song.
Again: Sum-mer-time and . . . This season's dress—
hospital green. But her veil—a fuchsia spirit.   *Christine Rhein*

Mary's tip: Don't say we died "fighting a courageous battle," spirit
unbowed. Don't sport pins signaling "awareness," don't book
tickets for charity-auction-banquet noblesse oblige. Don't dress
incredulous linebackers in pink cleats; claim envy for our fear-
lessness, admiration for our grace; de-compose us in a drippy song
of Spirit's brave skiff aimed shoreward. A slab is no damn port.   *Angela Ball*

Was she adrift . . . her port . . . somehow spirited
away? Melodious song . . . number 342, maroon book . . .
"Be not afraid" . . . banish fear . . . select a dress . . .   *Patricia Smith*

It has been an exhilarating run, and it isn't over yet: we need a title.

Or perhaps not: sometimes a generic title, the name of the form itself, seems to fit better than anything else. Case in point: one of the most celebrated sestinas in the language is Elizabeth Bishop's "Sestina." Which reminds me to remind you of the extraordinary popularity that the sestina has enjoyed since the aggressive turn toward modernism one hundred years ago.

I have, in fact, long nursed the idea of doing a historical anthology of the sestina in English. It would begin with Sir Philip Sidney's double sestina, "Ye Goatherd Gods." It would include sestinas by Kipling and Swinburne but would come into its own with the twentieth century: Ezra Pound's martial sestina in medieval accents ("Sestina: Altaforte"), T. S. Eliot's variant on the sestina form in *Four Quartets*, and a trio of sestinas by W. H. Auden ("Paysage Moralisé"), Elizabeth Bishop ("A Miracle for Breakfast"), and John Ashbery ("The Painter"), each of which illustrates the strategy of using five end words from one paradigm and the sixth from another. ("Prayer" performs this function in Ashbery's sestina—his first, written while he was still a Harvard undergraduate—just as "miracle" does in Bishop's.) James Merrill would be represented with a sestina whose ends words are one, two, three, four, five, and six, plus homonyms thereof, and there would be notable poems by Anthony Hecht, Donald Justice, and Alan Ansen. The last part of the book would have contemporary specimens, including our collaborative effort, in addition to works by Denise Duhamel, Catherine Bowman, Sherman Alexie, A. E. Stallings, Jonah Winter, Paul Muldoon, Deborah Garrison, Meg Kearney, Michael Quattrone, Terence Winch, Jenny Factor, and Laura Cronk. And surely we will want to highlight a poem from sestina maestro James Cummins's tour de force, *The Whole Truth*, a book consisting exclusively of sestinas that revolve around the exploits of Perry Mason, Della Street, Paul Drake, Hamilton Burger, and Lieutenant Tragg, the cast of the courtroom mysteries written by Erle Stanley Gardner and transferred to the small screen in the late 1950s with a cast headed by Raymond Burr. I can heartily recommend a fine anthology of contemporary sestinas edited by Daniel Nester, *The Incredible Sestina Anthology*.

I love the back-and-forth between and among "Next Line, Please" contributors and will contrive to come up with a contest that may engage us to the same extent. It won't be easy. Suggestions are most welcome.

And I would like to approve of the idea Paul Michelsen advocates—the idea of combining unchosen stanzas into alternative sestinas.

By midnight, Saturday, March 14, please submit a title for our collaborative effort—plus any thoughts you may have on how we may capitalize on the fine stanzas written for but not incorporated in our team sestina.

The Sestina Is Complete with "Compline"

March 17, 2015

The title that strikes me as the most elegant, succinct, and pertinent is "Compline," as proposed by Paul Michelsen. "Compline" is the Latin name for the night prayer, the final canonical prayer in the Catholic day, following Vespers. Our sestina is a prayer of sorts; it is endowed with religion and the spirit of divine immortality leavened by the occasional jest; and if readers don't recognize the title, all the better if they hunt it down in the dictionary or are moved to visit W. H. Auden's vastly underrated sequence of poems "Horae Canonicae." And if there are traces of "complete" and "complaint" in our title, so be it.

It was not an easy choice—I also liked "Her Hourglass a Prism" (Charise Hoge), "Mary, Singing" (Christine Rhein), "Uncertainty" (Patricia Smith), and LaWanda Walters's whimsical "How to Dress for Anything."

To all, my thanks, not only for the spirited effort resulting in a truly collaborative endeavor that can, I believe, stand on its own as an anthology piece of the future, but for the contagious enjoyment of the process. I am immensely gratified, too, by the compliments in my direction. If we are a team and I am the coach, well, that metaphor goes right to my head like a perfectly chilled, light-yellow drink consisting of top-shelf bourbon, lemon juice, and honey in equal measures, shaken and served in a rocks glass.

I shall do my best to contrive another contest that will spur the team to heights. But that may take me some time. Meanwhile, I have thought of prompts for the next couple of weeks, and I hope they will prove inspiring.

Here, then, is our complete sestina, written and titled over the past two months:

Compline

Finally the veins give out and they stick in a port
for the blood draws. Veins cave before the spirit.

Spirit caves before the voice stops the sing-song
of moan and groan that tolls all night like a book
of hymns without words. After a while even fear
caves, like a dress without a body or an address.

Diane Seuss

For life off-trend, beyond fashion, Mary K. wore no day dress,
only "gowns." She larked about chemo: "Any port
in a storm." When the doctor said, "Bad news," fear
was a vanity she dismissed: "Anodynes will keep my spirits
lit." She read scripture, began a memoir, a prose-poem book—
"not illness stuff"—but original woods, night-born foals, evensong.

Angela Ball

Visitors spark with lyrics of ballads, of songs,
a lamentation for the lack of redress
to tip the scale of slippery life. She jests, "Book
me a room with a courtyard and easy transport."
A smile dawns on her lips this cup won't pass; her spirit
a salve on tarnished will, her winsome style to balk at fear.

Charise Hoge

To speak of bravery is to speak of fear.
To lose oneself in singing is not to hear the song.
Awake in the night-dark, damp, she separated spirit
from Spirit, considered sightlines of corpse-dress.
Sometimes she laughed till tears came at the Colbert Report:
the good book is a good book, yes, but just a book.

James the Lesser

She thinks of her laden shelves, the thick textbooks
she trudged through, the boy she didn't marry, how fear
can squander a life. Above her heart, the pumping port
is silent. Again, she's free to hum any old song.
Again: Sum-mer-time and . . . This season's dress—
hospital green. But her veil—a fuchsia spirit.

Christine Rhein

Mary's tip: Don't say we died "fighting a courageous battle," spirit
unbowed. Don't sport pins signaling "awareness," don't book
tickets for charity-auction-banquet noblesse oblige. Don't dress

incredulous linebackers in pink cleats; claim envy for our fear-
lessness, admiration for our grace; de-compose us in a drippy song
of Spirit's brave skiff aimed shoreward. A slab is no damn port.   *Angela Ball*

Was she adrift . . . her port . . . somehow spirited
away? Melodious song . . . number 342, maroon book . . .
"Be not afraid" . . . banish fear . . . select a dress . . .   *Patricia Smith*

The Two-Line Poem

March 24, 2015

When I edited *The Oxford Book of American Poetry*, I discovered a whole genre of two-line poems—poems that make their point quickly and efficiently, with maximum clarity and economy and usually more than a soupçon of wit.

Let's write two-line poems for next week. The trick is, you need to write approximately ten of them to get one or two that are really terrific. So I encourage everyone to submit as many as five, optimally one on each of five successive days.

The most famous anthology piece is doubtlessly Ezra Pound's succinct plea for Imagism, "In a Station of the Metro": "The apparition of these faces in a crowd; / Petals on a wet, black bough." Each word is essential. The title situates us in the specific place; the first line gives us a close-up; the second line accomplishes the metaphorical transformation. Note that for Pound the urban modernist, the value remains on nature.

The funniest two-line poem is by my old friend, the late A. R. Ammons. It consists of nine words distributed evenly among the title and two lines. Here it is:

Their Sex Life

One failure on
Top of another

The double meaning of "failure" is sweet, and then the lining clinches the deal. The word "Top," capitalized (a very rare thing in Ammons's oeuvre), is the masterstroke.

The two-line poem can be an invitation to acerbic observation, as when Dorothy Parker, in "News Item," notes that "Men seldom make passes / At girls who wear glasses." How times have changed!

There is also the temptation to create an epigram. J. V. Cunningham was one of the best at this. Here is his "Epitaph for Anyone": "An old dissembler who lived out his lie / Lies here as if he did not fear to die." The poem's wit depends not only on the crucial pun that ends line one and starts line two but on the quality of lie and self-deception that the poet brilliantly captures.

I would also commend Charles Reznikoff's poem "The Old Man," a perfect illustration of objectivism: "The fish has too many bones, / and the watermelon too many seeds." The title is unpromising, yet the poem makes it come to life simply by giving us the man's point of view. Not an extraneous word, yet the voice of complaint is eloquent and convincing.

You are encouraged to write as many two-line poems as you can; discard the early efforts; try different styles and approaches and points of view. Have fun with it. All the examples given here, plus others, can be found in *The Oxford Book of American Poetry*.

Deadline: Saturday, March 28, midnight any time zone.

Wind and Ice

March 31, 2015

The two-line poem as a form seems to have evoked a good deal of imagery-driven verse, where the effort goes into finding the natural (or simply external and "objective") correlative to an emotional state.

First place is divided between Christine Rhein's "Grief, Like Ice":

Rain-pearls hang from branches,
tears that well but cannot fall

and Howard Altmann's "The Towering Wind":

So full of ivy
It empties the road.

There is a tie, too, for second place. Patricia Smith's "Alabama Mockingbirds" offers an internal rhyme—"morning" and "mocking"—that makes and mocks its own music:

Early morning chorus
all mocking birds

Ethelbert Miller, in a two-line poem inspired by Langston Hughes, expresses his feeling for his predecessor in the end words of the lines:

Langston Hughes knew rivers
I keep learning how to swim

Honorable mention: Charise Hoge's "Intimate Stranger":

The smile is no secret stash of happiness.
It's the turn of the world playing across his face.

In describing the two-line poem last week, I mentioned some modern American examples. Among great British poets, the master of the couplet—Alexander Pope (1688–1744)—has a brilliant two-line poem that sums up a rationalist century's attempt to reconcile science and religion: "Nature and nature's laws lay hid in night / God said: 'Let Newton be!' and all was light."

I'll have a new competition for us next week.

Let's Assemble a Cento

April 7, 2015

Starting this week, let's assemble a cento. The word "cento" was "Word-smith's" word of the day on March 14, and you can read their write-up online, replete with links to a cento John Ashbery wrote, as well as one that I put together for *The New York Times Book Review* upon completing *The Oxford Book of American Poetry* in 2006.

In the *Times* article, I do my best to present a succinct history of the cento, a poem consisting of lines culled from other poems—usually, but not invariably, poems from poets of earlier generations. Historically, the intent was often homage, but it could and can be lampoon. The modern cento has an altogether different rationale and flavor. It is based on the idea that in some sense all poems are collages made up of other people's words; that the collage is a valid method of composition, and even an eloquent one, as T. S. Eliot shows in "The Waste Land." Remember Eliot's motto: "Immature poets imitate; mature poets steal."

This is what I propose we do over the next four to six weeks.

For week one, let's come up with the first four lines of our cento. How? My recommendation is that you assemble on your desk four poetry books—or possibly one anthology—that you like. The poems can differ widely. Step two: choose one line from each of the four poems. You can do this arbitrarily (picking a line at random from page 25 of each volume, for example) or deliberately (recalling a favorite passage—perhaps one you underlined or otherwise noted). Step three: after writing down the lines, play with their order. Run them backward. Maybe line two would work better as line three. Don't worry overmuch about making sense. Sometimes, as Alice learns in Wonderland, if you take care of the sounds, the sense will take care of itself.

Rhyme can work: my "Cento: The True Romantics," a rhymed sonnet lifted from the romantic poets, has an honored place in my new book, *Poems in the Manner Of.* But rhyme is far from essential.

The winning entry will be our first four-line stanza. We can follow with two more such stanzas plus a closing couplet, or with three more aiming at a fearlessly symmetrical sixteen-line poem.

Unlike the sestina, which looks so forbiddingly difficult and turns out to be so liberating, the cento looks easy but may prove more challenging than expected. Some practitioners feel free to tamper a little with the stolen line; some think that is cheating. It's up to you. It would be helpful if you named your sources.

Naturally, I hope you will find this an inspiring prompt. Deadline: midnight, Saturday, April 11.

Our Crowd-Sourced Cento, Stanza One: Ten Blind Nights

April 14, 2015

Some fine entries came in for the opening stanza of our crowd-sourced cento—a concept and a phrase I like all the more because, in a sense, every cento is "crowd-sourced." And our project has the added virtue of spreading the word about what we are reading and who are the favorites to whom we turn at such a moment. I am delighted to see reading lists featuring such underrated greats as A. R. Ammons, Edna St. Vincent Millay, Joseph Ceravolo, Louise Bogan—not to mention Shakespeare, Blake, Thomas Hardy, and T. S. Eliot.

I wavered among three or four top candidates before choosing this quatrain by Paul Michelsen:

The wheels of a darkness without pain
Ten nights, without missing the stupid eye of the lighthouses
Ten blind nights free of idiot guiding flares
And in the silence, drips and cackles—taciturn, luxurious.

Sources by line, as identified by Michelsen:

Frank Stanford, "The Light the Dead See"
Arthur Rimbaud, "The Drunken Boat," translated by Wallace Fowlie
Arthur Rimbaud, "The Drunken Boat," translated by Martin Sorrell
Rosemary Tonks, "The Sofas, Fogs, and Cinemas"

Both lines two and three are translations of the following line: "Dix nuits, sans regretter l'oeil niais des falots!" The only "cheat" in these lines is the dropping of the end punctuation on lines 2 and 3.

Picking two different renderings of the same line from Rimbaud's "Le Bateau ivre" struck me as ingenious—and the maneuver works so well in context. Kudos, Paul.

Tied for the top runner-up slot are stanzas by Aaron Fagan and Berwyn Moore. Here is Aaron's. The disjunctions are arresting, yet the first three lines flow smoothly—and then A.R. Ammons's line comes along as if from an entirely different paradigm, pointing us in a fruitful new direction (and reminding us to read ARA's late masterpiece, *Garbage):*

The whole livery line
and the hitherto frowning moon fawns and
should take me and take you into their balloon,
garbage is spiritual, believable enough

Fagan identifies his sources as, in order:

Jean-Michel Basquiat
Frank O'Hara
ee cummings
A.R. Ammons

I love what Berwyn Moore does with her sources in this terrific stanza. Each line seems to prefigure what follows it:

What lover, what dreamer, would choose
farming: good Lord, worming tobacco, digging
to metaphysical newmown hay.
Hell must break before I am lost.

Sources:
Wallace Stevens, "Hymn from a Watermelon Pavilion"
A.R. Ammons, "Auditions"
Marianne Moore, "Tell Me, Tell Me"
H.D., "Eurydice"

For next time, we need another four-line stanza. How should it follow stanza one? I'm tempted to add a few other requirements—e.g., each candidate should include at least two words that appear in our initial stanza—but I leave it up to you. Please spread the word about our collaboration.

Deadline: midnight, Saturday, April 18.

Cento, Stanza Two: The Experience of Repetition

April 21, 2015

For the second stanza of our organic cento, I pick Berwyn Moore's candidate:

He cannot tell the rate at which he travels backwards,
the experience of repetition as death.
Not every man knows what he shall sing at the end.
Who made a ceremony of ash?

Sources:
Elizabeth Bishop, "The Man-Moth"
Adrienne Rich, "A Valediction Forbidding Mourning"
Mark Strand, "The End"
Pablo Neruda, "Sonata and Destructions"

The lines are singular, the phrases memorable—"repetition as death," "a ceremony of ash"—and they combine with the initial stanza in a way that stimulates and challenges the imagination.

Runner-up honors go to Charise Hoge, who starts by giving direction as to a tourist but widens the scope cinematically to the point where "horizontal" sounds as wide as the horizon:

You go straight ahead for about ten blocks
into cold, blue-black space,
alarming realm of the horizontal into
the resurrection of the morning.

Sources:
Mark Halliday, "Quartier"
Elizabeth Bishop, "In the Waiting Room"

Amy Clampitt, "The Cove"
Mary Oliver, "Hum, Hum"

Angela Ball shares the bronze medal with Poem Today. Here is Angela's effort, in which "night"—as fine as velvet, as claustrophobic as a "room in the earth"—claims our attention:

The night sits wherever you are. Your night
Sigh—the mocking just a stranger without humor
Night tumbles in velvet directions
Someone is digging a room in the earth

Sources:
Mahmoud Darwish, "Your Night Is of Lilac"
Nathalie Handal, "Alhandal y las Murallas de Córdoba"
Heidi Mordhorst, "Night Luck"
Quan Barry, "[nặng]"

The stanza proposed by Poem Today has the virtue of elaborating on the "pain" we had missed in the darkness. It also rhymes and adds another vote for Rimbaud among "sponsoring" poets. (Note: In the Rimbaud poem "Roman"—which I translated and titled as "Romance"—the line in question is "You're not too serious when you're seventeen years old," but I do not think these facts prejudiced me against Wallace Fowlie's perfectly acceptable rendering.)

Pain comes from the darkness and we call it wisdom—
Oh woe is me, t'have seen what I have seen—
Pain has an element of blank.
We aren't serious when we're seventeen.

Sources:
Randall Jarrell, "90 North"
William Shakespeare, *Hamlet*
Emily Dickinson
Arthur Rimbaud, "Novel," trans. Wallace Fowlie

Here, then, is our whole poem to date:

The wheels of a darkness without pain
Ten nights, without missing the stupid eye of the lighthouses
Ten blind nights free of idiot guiding flares
And in the silence, drips and cackles—taciturn, luxurious.

He cannot tell the rate at which he travels backwards,
the experience of repetition as death.
Not every man knows what he shall sing at the end.
Who made a ceremony of ash?

For next week, stanza three: four lines, and they can end the poem or set us up for a concluding quatrain or couplet.

Deadline: midnight, Saturday, April 25.

"Nobody Heard Him"

April 28, 2015

Among the excellent entries for this week, I found myself most captivated by Patricia Smith's stanza:

Nobody heard him, the dead man.
The dead are with us to stay.
They gave away the gift of those useful bodies.
Ash, ash—

    Sources:
Stevie Smith, "Not Waving but Drowning"
Charles Wright, "Homage to Paul Cézanne"
David Wagoner, "Their Bodies"
Sylvia Plath, "Lady Lazarus"

    I love how these lines follow the poem's first two stanzas—how they elaborate and complicate the themes of death, silence, and the "ceremony of ash."

    Among other strong contenders, let me single out this from Angela Ball:

Like the tucked sleeve of a one-armed boy
A magnate of kidnap
The truth is bald and cold
Our knowledge is historical, flowing, and flown.

    Sources:
W. S. Merwin, "When You Go Away"
James Tate, "A Vagabond"

Charles Simic, "The White Room"
Elizabeth Bishop, "At the Fishhouses"

A pleasure of the cento is that relatively familiar lines (Bishop's "Our knowledge") comingle with a compelling phrase one had not previously encountered—in this case, James Tate's amazing "magnate of kidnap."
Poem Today offers:

A concluding stanza (diminuendo)
Now let the cycle sweep us here and there.
Nor is there singing school but studying
ash on an old man's sleeve. Think
what houseflies have died in time.

    Sources:
H. D., "Sigil"
W. B. Yeats, "Sailing to Byzantium"
T. S. Eliot, "Little Gidding"
J. V. Cunningham, "Think"

Eliot's "ash on an old man's sleeve" goes together beautifully with the Yeats line from "Sailing to Byzantium."
So here is our cento to date (with stanzas by Paul Michelsen, Berwyn Moore, and Patricia Smith):

The wheels of a darkness without pain
Ten nights, without missing the stupid eye of the lighthouses
Ten blind nights free of idiot guiding flares
And in the silence, drips and cackles—taciturn, luxurious.

He cannot tell the rate at which he travels backwards,
the experience of repetition as death.
Not every man knows what he shall sing at the end.
Who made a ceremony of ash?

Nobody heard him, the dead man.
The dead are with us to stay.

They gave away the gift of those useful bodies.
Ash, ash—

For next week, let's bring our effort to a conclusion with a kick-ass couplet, rhymed or unrhymed. The idea of "repetition as death" seems to me to suggest a certain formal idea for the last two lines. But it is also possible to proceed by the logic of imagery ("ash"), metaphor ("ten blind nights"), or theme ("not every man knows what he shall sing at the end").

Deadline: midnight, Saturday, May 2.

Ashes, Ashes, All Fall Down . . .

May 5, 2015

To complete our collaborative cento, I opted for Jennifer Clarvoe's juxtaposition of lines from two great poems by Wallace Stevens:

One beats and beats for that which one believes.
The body dies; the body's beauty lives.

   Sources:
Wallace Stevens, "The Man on the Dump"
Wallace Stevens, "Peter Quince at the Clavier"

The leap from "Ash, ash—" to the line from "The Man on the Dump" seemed strangely captivating to me, and it is difficult to question the authority of the line from "Peter Quince at the Clavier."

   Second-place honors go to Poem Today, who explains that "the idea of 'repetition as death' [led] to the repetition of words and worlds" in these splendid lines from Howard Moss and Lord Tennyson:

The leaves' leavetaking overtaking leaves
The lucid interspace of world and world.

   Sources:
Howard Moss, "The Balcony with Birds"
Alfred Lord Tennyson, "Lucretius"

   Paul Michelsen comes in third with this exquisite conjunction of lines from Wilfred Owen and Joseph Ceravolo:

So secretly, like wrongs hushed-up, they went
Without a desperation to sing.

   Sources:
Wilfred Owen, "The Send-Off"
Joseph Ceravolo, "Soul in Migration"

   For the title of our effort I propose "All Fall Down," the ending of a familiar nursery rhyme that connects aptly with the theme of ashes.

   Here, then, is our cento, with stanzas assembled by Paul Michelsen, Berwyn Moore, Patricia Smith, and Jennifer Clarvoe:

All Fall Down

The wheels of a darkness without pain
Ten nights, without missing the stupid eye of the lighthouses
Ten blind nights free of idiot guiding flares
And in the silence, drips and cackles—taciturn, luxurious.

He cannot tell the rate at which he travels backwards,
the experience of repetition as death.
Not every man knows what he shall sing at the end.
Who made a ceremony of ash?

Nobody heard him, the dead man.
The dead are with us to stay.
They gave away the gift of those useful bodies.
Ash, ash—

One beats and beats for that which one believes.
The body dies; the body's beauty lives.

   Next Tuesday, May 12, we will have a compelling new contest. Please tune in then!

Similes Are Like Detours—or Shortcuts

May 12, 2015

Similes are underrated in contemporary writing. Well, maybe all rhetorical figures are underrated. The neglect of rhetorical devices, verse forms, rhyme, and other "adjuncts or ornaments" (as Milton would have it) is lamentable, but it does create a compelling opportunity for contemporary poets eager to embrace change and renew a past tradition. You can distinguish yourself from your peers just by making good use of similes.

A great simile opens a poem or narrative in a vertical way—it doesn't advance the argument or plot so much as it deepens it. Whether introduced by "like" or "as" or through some other means ("the size of a grapefruit"), the simile adds a complicating element even as it appears to clarify matters. It can resemble a detour—or a shortcut. It should surprise and should not repeat expressions already in use. Paradoxically, the simile can work to illustrate a thought or image—which is, after all, its stated function—yet it can overshadow the thought or image to which it was supposedly a subordinate element. Like the bridge in a jazz standard, it can surpass in beauty or inventiveness the primary melody, as happens in "Body and Soul" and "Skylark."

For brilliant similes, albeit in prose, I would recommend Mary McCarthy's *The Company She Keeps*—in which she tells us, for instance, that her heroine was the victim of a certain man's "conscience, as Isaac very nearly was of Abraham's." The religious and philosophical concerns of this author are front and center in a sentence that very surprisingly uses scientific means to explain a moral proposition: "To know God and yet do evil, this was the very essence of the Romantic life, a kind of electrolytical process in which the cathode and the anode act and react upon one another to ionize the soul." An enterprising professor could build half a college course around that sentence.

Nearly every page of A.J. Liebling's great book on boxing, *The Sweet Science,* can boast a refreshing, inventive simile or two. Example: "But Attell, who looks at you with cold eyes around his huge beak that is like a toucan's with a twisted septum, is not a sentimental man."

Your assignment for next Tuesday is to write a poem between four and eight lines long that (a) consists entirely of similes OR (b) lifts a simile from an unexpected prose source—such as *The Sweet Science* or *The Company She Keeps*—and goes to town with it. The poem need not rhyme or conform to an established formal meter.

Advice for option "a": concentrate on the similes and the flow of the writing and let the sense or meaning of the poem take care of itself. For option "b": for examples of how to incorporate a quotation in a poem, look at any volume by Marianne Moore.

Deadline: midnight, Saturday, May 16.

Like Dancing down the Aisle

May 19, 2015

So many good entries this week! They make me happy and confirm my belief that the simile—supposedly a subordinate figure of speech—can play a lead role in guiding a poem into being.

In the name of democracy and participatory reading, let me present my three favorites and ask you to cast your ballot.

As a longtime fan of Raymond Chandler who finds his similes and muted hyperboles irresistible, I may be an ideal reader for Angela Ball's "Chandleresque":

I felt like an amputated leg.
I felt I belonged here like a pearl onion on a banana split.
I felt like a thousand shabby lives.
I felt cold and wet as a toad's belly.
I felt like a showgirl's last pair of stockings.
I felt like the smile in your hip pocket.

The title makes an allusion to Hart Crane (who has a spectacular poem entitled "Chaplinesque"), and I recognize at least a few of the lines from Chandler's detective novels. I suspect many if not all of them are lifted straight from this master of the wisecrack, creator of Philip Marlowe. My one suggestion: vary the openings of the lines, even if just a little. I appreciate the use of anaphora, but I would suggest dropping "I felt" in line two and maybe changing "I felt" to something more surprising at the start of lines three and five.

Then there is Christine Rhein's "In the Waiting Room," the title of which echoes that of a celebrated late poem by Elizabeth Bishop:

Steady as a plow, an old woman crochets, her hook digging
in and out of rows, growing a gray blanket. The man beside her

watches the insistence of his own right arm, its tremor blaring
like the television, ad after ad for sunlit meadows, embraces.
When his name is called, she packs away the wool, the bundle
fuzzy, rough as hope. They stand, nudge each other forward,
shuffle, like they're skating on rusted blades or seized-up wheels.
But no, they're smiling. Like they're dancing down the aisle.

The last line is particularly compelling, buoyant in a way you wouldn't
have predicted from the first lines with their notable word choices:
"growing" a blanket, the "insistence" of a tremulous arm. The similes
in the last two lines clinch the deal, though I would respectfully suggest
substituting "as if" for "like" in both lines.

And I would like to commend Charise Hoge's "Fortune":

Forgiveness infallible as wings beating into arcing flight
sounding like a shudder of psalms circling
my rigid frame shaken unbolted like a trap door,
like a jaw dropped upon awe—awe like an anvil upon
which I am chiseled as the marble of myself, a marvel
casting off bitterness like sour bits of milk that churn
into butter like a taste of breaking the fast between us.

Here the acceleration of the lines gathers force; the relation of the
title to the first word is noteworthy, as is the beautiful internal rhyme of
"jaw" and "awe" in the pivotal fourth line.

I have something special contrived for next week's contest, but these
and other entries—by Millicent Caliban, Leonard Kress, Paul Michelsen,
Berwyn Moore, and LaWanda Walters—may persuade me to return to
the simile (and to other neglected figures of speech) very soon.

"In my end is my beginning"

May 26, 2015

"In my end is my beginning," T. S. Eliot wrote in *Four Quartets*. He meant something specific about circularity and the spiritual journey he was undertaking, but the line has more than one application, and I find it works to designate certain tactics or challenges that poets may employ to jump-start their imaginations. One such is to begin with a last line and then write the poem that leads up to it. Another—and the one I propose we use for this week's competition—is to retain the end words of an admirable poem, scrap the rest, and fill in the blank space with one's own poem.

Consider "Gare du Midi" by W. H. Auden. (You'll find it in a volume of Auden's selected poems and in some anthologies.) Only eight lines long, it implies a whole narrative with a sinister flavor suitable to Western Europe bracing for the gathering storm of World War II. The poem rhymes, but the rhymes are staggered—"contrived" in line three, for example, does not meet its mate until the last line of the poem. This allows the poem not only to evade expectation but almost to approach prose before fulfilling its obligations as verse. If you retain the end words, discarding the rest, this is what you get:

South,
face
contrived
mouth
pity.
case,
city
arrived.

Option two: For those who would be happier if the title of the poem were not revealed, here are the end words of another poem from the Auden canon:

after,
understand
hand,
fleets;
laughter
streets.

It is not necessary to retain Auden's punctuation. But be sure to give a title to your effort.

Incidentally . . . suggestions for future contests (another haiku perhaps? a poem based on a comparison? a cryptogram?) are always welcome, and you should know that I love it when people comment on the poems of others and on the exercise itself.

Deadline: midnight, Saturday, May 30.

"Homage to Auden"

June 2, 2015

Once again I find myself undecided when faced with three or four of the best compositions submitted in response to an Auden-centric prompt. To refresh memories, I suggested retaining the end words of either Auden's "Gare du Midi" or his "Epitaph on a Tyrant," scrapping the rest of the lines, and filling in the space with your own words.

I decided to divide first-place honors between Paul Michelsen's "Northeast of Eden" and LaWanda Walters's "Ingrown."

Paul Michelsen's "Northeast of Eden" is a tour de force. In addition to using the end words of "Gare du Midi" as the end words of his poem, Paul uses as his opening words the end words of "Epitaph on a Tyrant." Because the latter is only six lines long, and the new poem has to consist of eight lines in order to conform to the line length of "Gare du Midi," Paul cleverly adds the first word of Auden's title ("Epitaph") and the first word of his first line ("Tyrant") for the openings of his lines seven and eight. The maneuver of the dash and change of tense in line two suggest the poet has been reading Wallace Stevens. Here is "Northeast of Eden":

After things soured beyond hope my mind wandered South
Understand I have not—will not ever forget your face
Hand to the Heavens, the smithereens of my heart not contrived
Fleets take aim against me and the words that move my mouth
Laughter lunges forward like a reflex such as pity
Streets of tears turn confetti back to anonymous briefcase
Epitaph for the long lost soul of a lover and her city
Perfection existed somewhere once, the repo team arrived.

LaWanda Walters's "Ingrown" begins strongly—using "like" to signify a simile (a direction can resemble "a person's face") and as a vernacular equivalent of "for example" ("a direction—like South"). Our attention is sustained by an unfamiliar but interesting term—"Wardian case," named after the London doctor who invented it, refers to a type of sealed container for plants—and by a reference to a song from the 1960s. It adds to the poem's flavor that the last name of Gene Pitney—who sang "A Town Without Pity"—rhymes with "pity" and includes the word anagrammatically.

How odd that a direction—like South—
takes on meaning like a person's face.
After I had my half-Jewish children I contrived
ways never to return. Something about the mouth
of my grandfather I had seen sometimes. "A Town Without Pity"
sang Gene Pitney when I was twelve. A Wardian case
keeps curiosities, strange plants alive. We eluded that city,
hungry as a gingerbread house for my children to arrive.

Honorable mention goes to Berwyn Moore for her superb paraphrase of "Epitaph on a Tyrant." Her poem is entitled "Epitaph on a Housekeeper":

Cleanliness, of a sort, was what she was after,
And the ditties she composed were tough to understand;
She spotted pretension like dust on a gloved hand,
And was hardly enthralled by Armani or fleets
Of Fraser yachts; when she cried, politicians erupted in laughter,
And when she died, schoolboys flicked their butts in the streets.

Cheryl Whitehead's "Bound for Glory" also deserves commendation. The first five lines in particular are beautifully economical.

What became of the South
and its ruddy red face
where strange institutions contrived
a pretty mouth
that spoke without warmth? Pity
the place that let its blues tromp off, with guitar case

slung over its shoulder, to some Northern city.
"The train done brought me," the bluesman yelped when he arrived.

It has now been thirteen months since we initiated "Next Line, Please." I am glad that participants feel that it has been a success—inspiring in several ways. I agree, not only because I am committed to the use of prompts and exercises as a way of generating poems, but also because we are making creative use of the new electronic media. The back-and-forth among contributors reinforces the conviction that the lonely work of the poet is easier to bear when you have friends who can subordinate their natural competitiveness to the ideals of mutual support and constructive criticism.

As I listen to my favorite singer sing "South
of the Border," a smile dances on my face,
and I vow to do my best to contrive
a stimulating prompt that will inspire us to open our mouths
and sing. We shall banish self-pity.
Better than a case
of pale ale, in country or city,
is the pleasure of being there when we've arrived.

Poems and Secret Messages

June 9, 2015

In addition to their stated messages, some poems have secret messages embedded in them—sometimes reinforcing the point, sometimes at cross purposes with it.

Perhaps the most common way of concealing a message, whether subversive or not, is by use of an acrostic. And the most common acrostic involves the opening letters of the lines, which can spell out "I love you" or the poet's name or the name of the beloved or some imperative or other ("let's do it").

The way to do it is to start with the phrase and type it out vertically, then fill out the lines. Thus, and strictly from the top of my head, spur of the moment:

"Look out." But the admonition comes too late.
Every day brings danger, usually unforeseen.
There is only one remedy for this life of accidents.
So what are we to do? The enemy lines up.

Dread disease, car crash, gunshot wound, take your pick:
Our fate is sealed. It's just a matter of when.

I believe the evidence is incontrovertible.
The secret is out. Meet me at seven. You know where.

Try it. No need to boldface the opening letters. It is also possible to be even trickier—to use the last letters of the lines, for example. But let's keep the poem to twelve lines or under, OK?

Note: This week's short deadline is midnight, Friday, June 12.

"Conscience versus Consequence"

June 16, 2015

To say I am impressed with the ingenuity on display in this week's entries is to risk understatement. I'll just say that the decision to pick a winner gets more difficult each week—and that the association of poetry and secrecy remains a fruitful one.

I opted for a tie this time between two acrostic poems that could not be less alike: Christine Rhein's clandestine investigation of secrets and Millicent Caliban's high-spirited tip of the cap to the nation that was born on the fourth of July.

Here is Christine's poem, with its fine pugilistic metaphor ("a boxing match: / Conscience versus Consequence"), its blending of innuendo and implication, the way the lines themselves seem to "sneak and slither":

Keeping It to Yourself

Taste it each morning—tar in your teacup, dust on the milk—
How thick it grows, how brash. Hear it sneak and slither,
Edging its way across the floor, the walls, your back.

See it land atop your windshield, belly pinned against
Every turn, your signal's tick, tick, tick. It's a boxing match:
Conscience versus Consequence, your referee heart
Running in circles. Racing. How long can you hide it,
Easing it onto your half of the bed, its crashing weight at
Two a.m., at four. How long can it sing you back to sleep?

And here is Millicent's satirical, critical, yet finally affirmative "Poem for the 4th of July":

All you can eat, buffet or drive thru.
Made here (or make it anywhere?)
Equal all men are created and women, who may or may not be LGBT.
Rights unalienable,
Indivisible with liberty and justice for all.
Can do? Yes we can. Still.
Aspirational we remain.

But I cannot leave unmentioned Charise Hoge's mysterious poem with its anagrams ("trial" and "trail"), its framing rhyme ("Undone" and "all one"), its smart use of prefixes ("Underfoot" and "Understand"), the way the words rearrange themselves, so that "tread" gives birth to "red." The mysteries of this brilliant five-line effort are not to be quickly solved:

Undone by trial of trail cresting full sun.
Letters approach incantation chasm imaginative.
Underfoot red dirt decorates hem, cakes tread of soles.
Rim of rock, circling the ancestors' wholly baked faith:
Understand your walk alone, al-one, is all one.

Then there is this tour de force from Paul Michelsen, which gives you the same message if you read the initial words of the lines or the end words (though the latter must be read from bottom to top).

From Sandface to a Kicker of Sand

From sounding out letters to fancying oneself a reader
one has a summer reading list ready, a
who's who and what's what of what's hot and what's not—
not luke warm, not ice cold, but blisters on bare feet—One whose who's who's
a blazing hot coal, an out-of-control inferno, but there's not one
poet on this list, there will be no poems to—
to keep the fire lit as you sit before the shore, even though just one poet,
one poem, can make a much better what's what, a
who's who with which you cannot lose, a win-win, a not-

not lose-lose to make the reader one whose who's who's
a better thing for having been charged with poetry—There must be one
reader—one reader who gets where I'm coming from.

Brandon Crist's brilliant submission is, in his words, a "tiered acros-
tic, which encodes a nested message horizontally as well as vertically."
It is entitled "F-Minus," but Charise Hoge is right to give it the grade
of A-plus:

Fresh embers ebb, lofting
agilely
toward inward depletion; erupting
ingots now subdue infinite depressions; earthen
grins reveal overflowing wonders in naive guise;
usurped power
evaporates as sentries yawn

Nor shall I leave unmentioned Patricia Smith's one-word-per-line cele-
brations of "prayer" and "thesaurus" and LaWanda Walters's poem "The
Christian Woman Who Bought Our House." LaWanda, with whom I share
a birthday (June 11), repeats words to admirable effect—punning on
them ("that woman who prayed, or preyed, / for it's all the same thing")
or subtracting a suffix to good advantage (as "fixtures" turns into "fix").

Your quizmaster is going on a brief hiatus but will return refreshed,
God willing, and armed with new prompts and challenges by Labor Day.
In the meantime, Angela Ball will run the show in my absence. Regu-
lar participants know Angela's work; she was instrumental, for example,
when we built our sestina. In addition to being a talented poet and dis-
tinguished professor, much loved by her students at the University of
Southern Mississippi, Angela is an imaginative editor, who has assembled
special issues of *Mississippi Review* and *Valley Voices*. I am looking forward
to her prompts, and I am confident that "Next Line, Please" will be in the
best possible hands. Please give her your support.

Thank you, all, for making these competitions so exemplary in every
sense!

Becoming an Obstructionist

By Angela Ball

June 23, 2015

I have the honor of standing in for David Lehman as quizmaster this summer, and I'm excited to greet the followers, both new and continuing, of "Next Line, Please."

Perhaps the toughest part of writing anything is not knowing where the next piece is coming from. In these few weeks, I hope to suggest some workable answers for this dilemma, and to encourage readers to create and collaborate—as they have done splendidly for the last several months with David as coach and mentor.

Our first prompt has its source in Lars von Trier's 2003 film, *The Five Obstructions*, in which von Trier asks a mentor, director Jørgen Leth, to serially remake his 1967 short film, *The Perfect Human,* in accordance with various crippling stipulations, or "obstructions," such as "no shot lasting longer than twelve frames," "set it in the worst place in the world," and so forth.

Your job this week is to "obstruct" eight to ten lines of any well-known poem, using one of the following changeups:

Make the speaker another character in the poem. For example, the "last duchess hanging on the wall" in Robert Browning's poem, "My Last Duchess," could replace the duke, with the new title "His Last Duchess"; Pound's famous adaptation "The River Merchant's Wife" might become "The River Merchant."

Or . . .

Reverse (fully or partially) the meaning of eight to ten lines of any well-known poem. Instead of Yeats's "rough beast slouching towards Bethlehem," we might have "a gentle spirit floating towards Scranton." This second idea is inherited from the wonderful poet and teacher Donald Justice.

Whichever obstruction you choose, the goal is to create a short poem (or the beginnings of one) that captures interest on its own and as an homage and/or parody of its source. Have fun, and remember to title your effort.

The deadline for this week's entries: midnight, Saturday, June 27.

Unfinished Business

June 30, 2015

I'm delighted by the wealth of terrific responses to last week's prompt, as well as by the continued spirit of mutual support and collaboration among the poets. First-place honors go to Patricia Smith for her "Cadavers 101-Indiana University," which I'll reprint here:

The bloated woman . . . her hair dyed with henna,
the color of a clay pot. Maybe you'll forget her
in spite of her disgusting tattooed body,
her multiple piercings—nose, lips, elsewhere . . .
Perhaps you'll forget him, too . . . beer-bellied,
his face a collage of scars.
Indeed, his expression even in death suggests brutality—
each scar a reminder of an encounter or some unfinished business.
Remember only this: Dead folks like these will pay your salaries.

Smith's obstruction of David Wagoner's "Their Bodies" uses the prompt tragi-comically, turning the exemplary into the disreputable while affirming the bodies' worth.

In second place we have Berwyn Moore's "For I Will Consider the Wind," with its deft transformation of Christopher Smart's famous poem into a new work that brilliantly shows "the way the wind ruffles and tatters what we think is ours." (For another poem that revisits Smart to brilliant effect, see Wendy Cope's "My Lover.") Honorable mentions go to Paul Michelsen's "Waving," Charise Hoge's "the how town downtowners," Allison Campbell's "The [Impatient & Ill Advised] Waking," Annette Boehm's "Thirteen Ways of Ignoring a White Rat," and LaWanda Walters's "Waving, Not Drowning."

To begin this week's prompt, I'd like to direct you to the first stanza of Kenneth Koch's much-anthologized poem "You Were Wearing," where we encounter an Edgar Allan Poe printed cotton blouse, a John Green-leaf Whittier hair clip, and a pair of "George Washington, Father of His Country, shoes."

In this prescient poem from 1962, we are flung into a world in which famous artistic and political identities brand ordinary objects. The family seems perhaps a bit unhinged, or at least starstruck. The objects' borrowed brilliance is only a veneer, as the scraped-off blue enamel reminds us. But wait—the shoes belong to the speaker, who is implicated in the craze. The deadpan specificity of reference—"George Washington, Father of His Country, shoes"—suggests an ad for a prestige collectible. At the same time that it showcases its "products," the poem runs a parallel narrative of young love, to great comic effect.

There may be no "Edgar Allan Poe" blouse, but there is surely a T-shirt, tote bag, and mug. Soccer players score and deflect goals while their shirts sell plane tickets and automobiles. Tradition to the contrary, it may be only a matter of time until American football players' uniforms become billboards. We can bemoan this as crass—or we can, in the words of Irving Berlin, "Face the Music and Dance."

For this week, try writing an eight- to ten-line poem featuring at least three products, real or invented. Feel free to emulate and/or depart from Kenneth Koch's method. Most of all, enjoy the playfulness inherent in the idea. Title your poem, and post it no later than midnight (eastern time), July 4—Independence Day.

Product Placement

July 7, 2015

What a selection of product poems to choose from! A wonderful literary catalogue could be composed, offering "a Stevie Smith Inner Tube," "Whitman Unisex Beach Towels," and "Emily Dickinson Fly Paper." After much deliberation, I decided that Annette Boehm's "Costermonger" and Paul Michelsen's "A Day at the Beach" tie for first place.

Costermonger

For the man of the house: the Dylan
Thomas Travel Flask, to carry good spirits
along at all times. Lined thickly with pewter
this beautiful piece will serve well
when he's done you disservice.

We carry, too, these exquisite Woolf
cigarette holders, cocktail & dinner
length, fashioned from Bakelite
with a discrete asbestos inlay. With these
it doesn't matter what Milady smokes.

We vouch for Dickinson's Fly Paper—
It's effective! It's the arsenic, like her lace:
near invisible, but still enough to ensure
through the whole, well-kept house
the peace and quiet you so desire.

The broad humor of the "Dylan Thomas Travel Flask" shades into the menacing yet attractive house of Dickinson. The poem's unctuous product descriptions are both suggestive and entertaining. I particularly admire the epigrammatic close of stanza one: "will serve well / when he's done you disservice."

I chose Paul Michelsen's "A Day at the Beach" because of the way its products spring to life as they are deployed—one of the beauties of the Koch poem that inspired the prompt:

A Day at the Beach

I'd already applied the Dickinson sunscreen
And spread out the Whitman unisex beach towels
"Please pass the Kafka spray—damn these mosquitoes,
So rude coming under our Crusoe umbrella.
Hand me my phone—I have texting to do.
Damn you, autocorrect! Your caps are a slap—does context mean nothing?"
(i was quoting cummings whose face on my phonecase was proof he did not
    approve)
Correcting corrections, when I should've been kissing and patching things up
    with you
I'm sorry I didn't notice you waving, my Love, from your hissing Stevie Smith
    inner tube.

One of Michelsen's funniest effects (out of many) is achieved by clinching "patching things up" with the hilarious "Stevie Smith inner tube."

Runner-up honors go to a completely different take on the prompt, LaWanda Walters's "Name Brands," with its confident, jazzy narrative in which products embody and illuminate both relationships between characters and spots of time.

Name Brands

You were always carrying THE WAY OF ZEN
in the back pocket of your Levi's,
and we were drinking Gallo Burgundy
and you couldn't believe I hadn't heard
of Van Gogh, and Mother drove you
up to Penland, where you met Paulus Berenson
and that was the beginning—

what my mother did, researching Penland
like she used to find out about music schools
for my sister, which led to all those rich people
from Esalen, that older woman giving you sixty acres
if you'd live on her place on the mountain between Ukiah
and Mendocino, but you wanted to have me, too,
so we drove up to her paradise for a while,
me skinny dipping with her and you that first day
to prove something I didn't quite understand
until I picked up that book by Alan Watts
in her living room, "No, you're not at a place yet
to get this." And then she gave me what looked
like a fat comic book for kids,
BE HERE NOW by Baba Ram Dass,
and everyone but me had a Coors beer.

For next week, the task is what I'll term "poetry of instruction." Many famous poems contain instructions, direct or implied. For instance, there's Elizabeth Bishop's "One Art" ("Lose something every day"), and Theodore Roethke's "The Waking" ("I wake to sleep, and take my waking slow"). Some incorporate "found" material from sources like old cookbooks, textbooks, "how-to" books, and the like. Advice from another age is often humorous. As in the now-obvious fakery of old films' driving scenes, a gap yawns between language and the conditions it seeks to address.

Instructions can be sinister, brandishing an implied "or else," as in some advice I long ago received on dating: "Always keep one foot on the floor." Here, the balance between information and mystery is skewed greatly toward mystery, which, if not a great thing for life, can be a very good thing for poetry.

I once used a children's health text—its title and author now lost to me—to write a poem called "Improve Your Posture." Here's the ending:

Avoid keeping your hands
and arms behind your back
as if impersonating
an armless statue.

Instructions are haunted by the specter of destruction, like the Age of Reason by its madhouses. Often, they assert power—the more anonymous, the more aggressive. Often, advice supports social norms later proven despicable. All of these features make for illuminating repurposing as poetry.

I propose that you write a poem eight- to sixteen-lines long consisting of instructions, found or original. Title your poem, and submit it no later than midnight eastern time on Saturday, July 11.

Making Groceries

July 14, 2015

This phrase, as you may know, is the New Orleans idiom for "going food shopping." I like it for the much-deserved credit it gives the shopper. This week's winning poem, by Christine Rhein, has as its title a reversal of Randall Jarrell's brilliant *Sad Heart at the Supermarket:*

Do Not Cry in the Supermarket

Do not imagine yourself a lab mouse, racing down
towering aisles, each turn another decision. Don't listen
to the light jazz, even in Produce—fruits and vegetables
heaped to verge of avalanche. Do not consider the squash,
how to disguise it so your family might eat it. Never mind
the tests of will—a dozen ingredients needing chopping
versus soup in cans needing pouring, name brand
versus bargain, Oreos versus no Oreos. Do not get sick
of chicken. Don't think twice about detergents—neon-loud
boxes shouting "Environmentally Kind" or about your favorite
soap—for years—the flowering promise: "Softer, younger-
looking skin." Above all, ignore the man ahead of you in line—
how handsome he is—dressed for Saturday night, swinging
his basket of red wine, French bread, two T-bone steaks,
and a glistening carton of Vanilla Caramel Fudge ice cream.

The poem's rhetoric is brilliantly simple and simply brilliant: its assertions turn themselves inside out serially, finally leaving us at the mercy of the "glistening carton" of three-pronged temptation.

In second place, we have Berwyn Moore's "Story of the Bear":

I trudge through snake grass to get home where my mother
has made soup with chunks of raw meat and fish. When

n out with my fingers, she smiles, but when
. ...e foil-wrapped candy, she scolds me and tells
me to hold each piece in my spoon and shake it gently
until the silver paper falls off. I try to tell her my story
of the bear, but she shushes me, so I leave her at the table
talking to the soup and walk outside. The points of stars
take shape, Ursa Major climbing across the sky. And across
the road, beyond the gray breath of fear, a grizzly bear
spanks the air with huge paws, a cub nuzzling her flanks.
I crouch behind a bush to watch, and when the child
in my womb stirs—the first time—I understand what
I was admonished for: this story of the bear, this fierce
possession, how it sends us away, then pulls us back
to bad soup and hard chairs, famished and forgiving.

The picture the poem composes of the mother grizzly pawing at Ursa Major strikes me as wonderful, as well as how the human mother and child play off against the ursine sow and cub.

Third place is captured by another mother-daughter entry, Charise Hoge's "Wash," with its surprise note for a "willowy daughter":

No perfumes or dyes, for sensitive skin.
May irritate eyes, keep from reach of children.
Sorting serves to distort the all at once-ness:
lifting covers for a yet to be known lover,
tugging at last season's pants, button hole evaded,
folding up one thought to air another,
eyeing a secretly passed note pocketed
in shorts—saying it's time for a willowy
daughter to do her own laundry.

Finally, an enthusiastic honorable mention is due to both "A Lesson in Economy from France, 1962" and "Aspects of Loneliness," by Paul Michelsen. How delightful to be introduced to *It's a Weird World*, by the poet's uncle, Paul Stirling Hagerman—not to mention Anthony Greenbank's somewhat less convincingly titled *The Book of Survival*.

For this week: Road Trip.

In some parts of rural America, long-ago motorists would pass a slanted roof painted with an invitation like "See Mammoth Cave" or a barn wall with "See Natural Bridge." Each painted structure seemed to inhabit a limbo between its actual location and the scenic monument. The very idea that people would follow this command, undertake a journey of some hundreds of miles on the strength of three painted words, is a kind of magical thinking hard to imagine happening in Europe: an alpine barn painted with the Swiss-German words "See the Hanging Gardens of Babylon." In that spirit, let's travel together, not by the usual means but by what John Keats called "the viewless wings of poesy."

I propose that the famous adventurer Lord Byron start us off by lending the form of his epic, picaresque, and unfinished long poem, *Don Juan*.

Here's the first stanza of that poem's first canto:

I want a hero: an uncommon want,
When every year and month sends forth a new one,
Till, after cloying the gazettes with cant,
The age discovers he is not the true one;
Of such as these I should not care to vaunt,
I'll therefore take our ancient friend Don Juan—
We all have seen him, in the pantomime,
Sent to the devil somewhat ere his time.

All that you need emulate is the form—one iambic pentameter eight-line stanza rhyming *abababcc*. Off rhymes and extra or missing feet can add a welcome playfulness.

Other choices to inform our poem (eventually a six-stanza canto) will emerge as we go. We may have no hero or several; may navigate the present and/or the past, literature and/or life; or create a postmodern mash-up of contexts. What might a contemporary *Canterbury Tales* look like? Or an updated version of John Steinbeck's *Travels with Charlie*, in verse?

Antonio Machado will provide our motto: "Traveller, there is no road—we make our road by going."

Entries must be submitted by midnight, eastern time, on July 18.

The Trip Begins

July 21, 2015

What a luxury of choices for the start of our communal canto. Although any one of these fine entries would make an intriguing beginning for our expedition, let's go with Charise Hoge and her "gypsy soul":

On a Caravan of Dreams

The trip begins without a sign that's hung.
The mark may lie within your palm a line
a psychic knew before your time was sung.
She saw the span of dissonance: you pine
to scale a chart, depart where others clung;
refuse the map, forget reviews unkind.
My year of birth your cry of "Something Else!!!!"
A gypsy soul keeps nothing on the shelf.

This stanza is a rich starting point, both in its own special "something else" and in its ekphrastic (art speaking to art) connection to *Opening a Caravan of Dreams*, a 1985 album by the saxophonist Ornette Coleman and his Prime Time ensemble. This album references Fort Worth's artist-run performing arts center and nightclub, The Caravan of Dreams, christened in 1983 with a Coleman performance. The phrase "caravan of dreams" originates from *One Thousand and One Nights*, in which individual narratives both gather within and illuminate the frame story of brave Scheherazade, who saves herself and the kingdom's women with stories, each night mesmerizing her captor with a suspended tale, a veiled future.

Hoge's stanza demonstrates the nature of art as eternal return. Jazz builds on jazz—but Coleman's genius sax and this new stanza unsettle the score.

Second place goes to another ekphrastic stanza, Berwyn Moore's linked collage of incidents based on Pieter Bruegel the Elder's painting, "Netherlandish Proverbs":

Only the sun holds still, over the bay,
its blue penumbra both morning and night.
The town itself bristles, a busy spray
of flaw and folly. One man, full of spite,
flings feathers to the wind; a woman sways
her friend with gossip. Yet no one incites
the other to anger. There hangs the knife,
and there sighs the man with his cheating wife.

The description of the town as "a busy spray / of flaw and folly" is a revelation, with "spray" working overtime to make an image of what would otherwise be invisible. Though passionate, the scene is compellingly inconclusive: "no one incites," "There hangs the knife," "there sighs the man." Only a rhyme couples "knife" with "wife."

Third-place honors go to Jordan Sanderson's arresting "A Goat in Tennessee":

In the road a goat stood munching a scarf
Blown from the neck of a pilot. The fingers
Of a lady's black glove marked with a heart
Clutched the goat's left horn. It seemed de rigueur
To swerve, but someone had left a glass jar
On the shoulder. Our tire ruined, we lingered.
We followed the goat when it bleated, for
We were somewhere we had never been before.

This charmingly omnivorous goat reminds me of Louis Simpson's famous dictum at the start of "American Poetry"—that it must be able to stomach and digest "Rubber, coal, uranium, moons, poems."

There's much to get from Sanderson's goat—the philosophical jeu d'esprit of Wallace Stevens, the elegant anarchy of past avant-gardes. I hope for another chance to follow its bleats to somewhere else I've never been before.

I also covet a ticket for Paul Michelsen's "Greyhound," this week's honorable mention:

An odyssey begins on Greyhound bus
The driver barely looks to say hello
These passengers may look worse-off than us
As tattered as the bags tossed down below
No single one looks like someone you'd trust
Not one resembling anyone I know
But each of us is picturing the end
Though none of us is going where we've been

This bus seems quintessentially American—and also poemlike. Imagine the passengers as words, the aisle as caesura. Destination a title printed on a roll of paper hurriedly wound forward.

As our own working title, let's recruit "Caravan of Dreams." In proposing a second stanza, aim to touch some aspect of the first but also to depart from it—improvising onward in a jazz spirit. At the same time, hold to our eight-line stanza with its flexible iambic base, and its *ababababcc* rhyme scheme. Keep in mind what Ornette Coleman once said of his band members: "I don't want them to follow me. I want them to follow themselves, but to be with me." Submit your stanza no later than midnight eastern time, July 25.

Antipodal Star

July 28, 2015

The second stanza of our "caravan of dreams" will be Berwyn Moore's:

Refuse the map. Forego the sturdy shoes.
Shrug off the ragged water of the past.
Your antipodal star riffs like the blues.
Step double-time across the bones and vast
landscapes of asphalt and stubble. He woos
you still, and waits, declares he'll be the last.
His words flutter like ashes in the wind.
For once, run away, free, undisciplined.

Here we are enjoined to forget our predecessor—a perilous venture for any artist—and to strike out solo over "asphalt and stubble." "His words flutter like ashes in the wind," a seductive beauty we must refuse.

In second place, we have Patricia Smith, whose stanza, like our first, takes Ornette Coleman as its muse:

This troupe of writers—phraseology
to encourage while collaborating—
searching for our shared "harmolodies,"
rhyme and rhythm in our versifying,
connections made, a few perhaps off-key,
that faultless euphony we are seeking.
No Pulitzer awaits our "Sound Grammar"—
this caravan of dreamers, raconteurs.

I admire how Smith has joined our mission to Coleman's through his eccentric "harmolodies" and "Sound Grammar"—proof that art is one project, using and breaking rules to arrive at both self and transcendence.

Tying for third place are Paul Michelsen and Jordan Sanderson. Michelsen's stanza is ambitiously pan-cultural:

The others dream their dreams of Golden Fleece,
The gods and goddesses they hope to marry
A different psychic said we'd go back East
She told a tale of constellation Aries
To figure what/what not to take with me
Refuse to use the maps my cellphone carries
My keen affinity for fairies and
A trust in Warwick and her psychic friends

Here, the connection of cellphones to divination seems both natural and anachronistic.

I suggest that you consult last week's column for the maiden appearance of Sanderson's allusive goat guide:

Late that night or early that morning, we
Found the goat had delivered us to the site
Of a wreck and wandered into the trees.
Survivalists we were not, but we dived
In and divvied up the things we might need:
A prosthetic tongue, a twinge of twilight,
A book of matches to use as moorings
Should the blown world become too alluring.

I propose a new muse for this week, the Polish poet Adam Zagajewski. In such a poem as "En Route," translated by Clare Cavanagh, Zagajewski alternates between inner and outer weathers. Along the way he interposes the mundane. To a woman interrupting his reverie, he says: "this is the nontalking compartment." In one brilliant line, Zagajewski personifies a month, and dramatizes how landscape harbors transformation: "October was hiding in the weeds." The hawk appears, part of the natural order, but also in devastating contrast to us and our daily commute, a prison sentence never lifted.

Here is our canto thus far:

Caravan of Dreams

The trip begins without a sign that's hung.
The mark may lie within your palm a line
a psychic knew before your time was sung.
She saw the span of dissonance: you pine
to scale a chart, depart where others clung;
refuse the map, forget reviews unkind.
My year of birth your cry of "Something Else!!!!"
A gypsy soul keeps nothing on the shelf.

Refuse the map. Forego the sturdy shoes.
Shrug off the ragged water of the past.
Your antipodal star riffs like the blues.
Step double-time across the bones and vast
landscapes of asphalt and stubble. He woos
you still, and waits, declares he'll be the last.
His words flutter like ashes in the wind.
For once, run away, free, undisciplined.

For our third stanza, we'll keep to our form: eight lines rhymed *ababababcc*. "Caravan of Dreams" is still a "working" title—that is, subject to change. Wear it lightly, and work toward your own balance of expectation and surprise. Submit your entries no later than midnight eastern time, Saturday, August 1.

Appaloosa Sky

August 4, 2015

Of this week's several fine offerings, I choose Jordan Sanderson's as
stanza three:

The sky was appaloosa, the town paint.
The electric train plucked by, and the sky
Was bone, and the wind fluted through its flank.
We emerged like half-notes from a horn sighed
Onto the slick stave of the riverbank,
Where even in our rapture we were shy.
A song yanked at our mouths like a bit.
Stampeding, we embraced its roan beat.

These lines arrest with their synesthetic melding of horses, weather,
and music both natural and human. "We," the lovers, are inseparable
from the song that enraptures and transforms. Paradoxically, it provokes
a stampede—but instead of breaking, the song's rhythm only increases
its hold. Unlike our first two stanzas, which occur in the present, this one
looks back; it could constitute either an interlude in our canto or a sign-
post forward.

For second place, I choose Fae Dremock's stanza, with its surprising
wordplay and its engine of panic that urges freedom but only retraces a loop:

Still we chug through monochrome—grey ash grown dark,
past ember and last arc of char, bird flight
once furl of silk, now canvas sheet and stark.
And we, astride cold fire, beat slow tonight.
But wake to hiss and cracks of trees that mark
again hot drought. "Run!" The flame burns right through
us. Run! Trail's ablaze! No maps—run wild!
By morning, a circle, worn flat. And guile.

Tied for third place are LE Goldstein's and Patricia Smith's entries. Goldstein's stanza delights in disjunction:

Leave your skin's shadow on baked stones
by the river. The pink dolphin
will sue her ex-boyfriends; they've grown
avocado-pit hearts, leering grins
that once bit her ear slits. I've known
these white moths for years. Ask the shy
child; strong roots can snap from one lie.

The oracular confidence of its voice, moving from surreal command, to prediction, to statement of fact, to adage, casts a disturbing spell.

Here is Smith's contribution, with its unexpected coupling of muse and stoplight:

To travel without baggage is a dream
recurring often times on sleepless nights
when dreams seem reality disguised. Perhaps
darkness frees the room of lurking fright.
You hear, "Venture out, capture, redeem
that tangible dream, baggage free, outright."
In the shadow stands the Muse awaiting
a greening of the stoplight. Wondering. . . .

These engaging lines affirm the value of venturing out but at the same hold "that tangible dream" suspect. They end daringly, with the tentativeness of "Wondering. . . ."

William Butler Yeats's "A Coat," written when the poet felt an imperative to strip and modernize his style, throws off the mantle of tradition—an important, particular tradition that he helped to revive—and makes vulnerability a radical virtue. "I made my song a coat," he begins and tells us how he embroidered it with mythologies. When fools make off with it, he instructs his song to let them take it. "There's more enterprise / In walking naked."

This credo, or something like it, is affirmed in our canto so far, though it doesn't shy from complication, and each stanza is longer than Yeats's entire poem:

Caravan of Dreams

The trip begins without a sign that's hung.
The mark may lie within your palm a line
a psychic knew before your time was sung.
She saw the span of dissonance: you pine
to scale a chart, depart where others clung;
refuse the map, forget reviews unkind.
My year of birth your cry of "Something Else!!!!"
A gypsy soul keeps nothing on the shelf.

Refuse the map. Forego the sturdy shoes.
Shrug off the ragged water of the past.
Your antipodal star riffs like the blues.
Step double-time across the bones and vast
landscapes of asphalt and stubble. He woos
you still, and waits, declares he'll be the last.
His words flutter like ashes in the wind.
For once, run away, free, undisciplined.

The sky was appaloosa, the town paint.
The electric train plucked by, and the sky
Was bone, and the wind fluted through its flank.
We emerged like half-notes from a horn sighed
Onto the slick stave of the riverbank,
Where even in our rapture we were shy.
A song yanked at our mouths like a bit.
Stampeding, we embraced its roan beat.

We're midway in our enterprise. Much has been determined; anything can happen. I look forward to the directions scouted for stanza four. We'll keep to our eight lines of flexible iambic pentameter, rhymed *ababababcc*. Submit your entries no later than midnight eastern time, Saturday, August 1.

Legato Dreams

August 11, 2015

Of all the lovely stanzas submitted this week, my choice is Patricia Smith's:

Accelerato, adagio—our soul
vacillating, forever wondering
what movement or coda might make the whole
emerge as that resolute rendering.
Welcoming transformations—staccato,
legato—all the while probing dreams
dreamed in the depths of our mind and heart,
curious—Are we ending . . . where to start?

 Musical Italian syncopates the lines, gives them jazz leaps, while at the same time announcing directives. The question "How do we play this?" is posed and answered in multifarious ways.

 Tied for second place are stanzas by Jordan Sanderson, Charise Hoge, and Fae Dremock. Here is Sanderson's:

Inshore, it's mostly croakers and hardheads,
But taste has always been a matter of
Development, and lightly do we tread
The shallows. Look how the swimmers scatter!
Our journey runs parallel to what's unsaid.
When we find a map, it is in tatters.
Someone who knows said, "Ghost crabs clean the beach."
We feast on the faint crumbs of la durée.

 The lovely, abrasive first line moves us into rich speculation. Indeed, "Our journey runs parallel to what's unsaid." The haunting yet matter-of-fact adage, "Ghost crabs clean the beach," initiates us into nature's mysterious practicalities.

Charise Hoge's stanza proposes a fierce interpersonal music:

A tangent season suddenly thudded
like heavy cloaks now soaked no longer warming.
We bristled to the corners of the bed.
My pulse decried the effort of a drumming
for steadiness—to improvise instead.
Rephrase the brush with dread, let loose repeating
whatever we said and follow the tune of raw
unguarded moments . . . stop rewinding flaws.

Her lines strike at the obsessive repetition that too often bars understanding.

Fae Dremock's stanza imagines a violent accident or crime that almost seems a birth:

Pushing past the rim of notefall
down blue glacier, fissure, black rock,
carabiners clipped . . . bodies sprawled
in plain sight. Two cut cords. The clock
beats back hard brandied nights. Recall—
a fallen moon. Wet earth. The hawk
we tracked through echoed, cloven heart,
dropped. We shuddered close, ripped apart.

I admire the energy and insistence of Dremock's staccato, dreamlike report.

Honorable mention goes to one of Paul Michelsen's stanzas, with its slap-happy exuberance and verve:

Dropped everything to go: fork, plate, food, mind,
friends, fam, eggs and Spam, French fries, even this:
The last egg in the carton. We might find
the hard way Humpty Dumpty's mighty pissed.
And as we went took out a Cyclops' eye,

then pissed on a very pissed off Phoenix.
Passed through every Athens, even in Ohio.
And then on to Harlem to play the Apollo.

Here is our canto thus far:

Caravan of Dreams

The trip begins without a sign that's hung.
The mark may lie within your palm a line
a psychic knew before your time was sung.
She saw the span of dissonance: you pine
to scale a chart, depart where others clung;
refuse the map, forget reviews unkind.
My year of birth your cry of "Something Else!!!!"
A gypsy soul keeps nothing on the shelf.

Refuse the map. Forego the sturdy shoes.
Shrug off the ragged water of the past.
Your antipodal star riffs like the blues.
Step double-time across the bones and vast
landscapes of asphalt and stubble. He woos
you still, and waits, declares he'll be the last.
His words flutter like ashes in the wind.
For once, run away, free, undisciplined.

The sky was appaloosa, the town paint.
The electric train plucked by, and the sky
Was bone, and the wind fluted through its flank.
We emerged like half-notes from a horn sighed
Onto the slick stave of the riverbank,
Where even in our rapture we were shy.
A song yanked at our mouths like a bit.
Stampeding, we embraced its roan beat.

Accelerato, adagio—our soul
vacillating, forever wondering

what movement or coda might make the whole
emerge as that resolute rendering.
Welcoming transformations—staccato,
legato—all the while probing dreams
dreamed in the depths of our mind and heart,
curious—Are we ending . . . where to start?

With two more stanzas to go, it's crucial both to reiterate preoccupations and also to prevision what our ending might disrupt and crystallize.

If you need an extra dose of inspiration, consider taking a look at James Tate's poem "The Vagabond." Tate describes the title figure as "an eyeball at a peephole / that should be electrocuted" as well as "a leper in a textile mill" headed for the guillotine.

Of Tate's work in general, Charles Simic has said, "Just about anything can happen next in this kind of poetry, and that is its attraction." Here, it is possible to both cultivate and resist synthesis. The poem is grounded by a central character, but flung in all directions by impulse. To borrow Tate's verb, I hope you "paradise" next week's stanza while keeping purchase on things like asphalt and bone.

Remember our malleable scheme—an eight-line stanza of approximate iambic pentameter, rhymed *abababcc*—and be sure to submit your stanza no later than midnight eastern time on Saturday, August 15.

Beautiful Land

August 18, 2015

For our penultimate stanza, I choose Jordan Sanderson's:

We said things like, "That's some beautiful land,"
Before we dreamed we were awake. We said,
"Caves are rhetorical questions about lost hands."
"Descent is the last good word," we chanted.
Up the road, an ice cream truck played canned
Music. Its shrill sweetness went to our heads.
Ants gravitated to the melting song.
We trailed after them. We could not go wrong.

Its foregrounding of the speech act interestingly parallels stanza four, in which musical terms create poetic music. Whereas Smith's stanza evokes grandeur, Sanderson's brings in an ice cream truck's gaudy tune. His "we" takes sure direction from ants, whose frenetic colonies seem to mimic human war. (On this subject, read E. O. Wilson, the world's expert on myrmecology.)

Tied for second place are fine stanzas by Patricia Smith and Paul Michelsen. Here is Smith's:

Our launching pad of shoe-shined shoes propelled
us into another dimension
where individual dream-world sounds meld
into a collective montage vision—
our ethereal vibrations emerged.
This caravan of artistic creation
journeys on. Our plight: the wane to fight,
to "rage against the dying of the light."

I admire how the stanza's first line combines humility with ambition, and how each line expresses our intent to band together against inertia. Its ending enlists Dylan Thomas's great villanelle, "Do not go gentle into that good night," for our common cause.

Here is Michelsen's stanza:

Sat on phone books, a stack of almanacs
Drove stolen ice cream trucks, a series of Priuses
From a room half filled with full-time lunatics,
frackedelic company heads obsessed with fine cheeses,
to ballrooms bustling with quantum mechanics—
Did the running man with men who thought they were Jesuses
We dosey doed with CEOs and hokey pokeyed
then turned our backs like Miles as we karaoked.

Michelsen takes a cue from our presiding genius, Lord Byron, in the satirical bent of his stanza, which skewers corporate culture as it travels a dancing route and ends in triumphant jazz and superimposed song. Indeed, who can fail to admire the swashbuckling rhymes of "Priuses" with "cheeses" and "pokeyed" with "karaoked"?

Here is our canto as it now stands:

Caravan of Dreams

The trip begins without a sign that's hung.
The mark may lie within your palm a line
a psychic knew before your time was sung.
She saw the span of dissonance: you pine
to scale a chart, depart where others clung;
refuse the map, forget reviews unkind.
My year of birth your cry of "Something Else!!!!"
A gypsy soul keeps nothing on the shelf.

Refuse the map. Forego the sturdy shoes.
Shrug off the ragged water of the past.

Your antipodal star riffs like the blues.
Step double-time across the bones and vast
landscapes of asphalt and stubble. He woos
you still, and waits, declares he'll be the last.
His words flutter like ashes in the wind.
For once, run away, free, undisciplined.

The sky was appaloosa, the town paint.
The electric train plucked by, and the sky
Was bone, and the wind fluted through its flank.
We emerged like half-notes from a horn sighed
Onto the slick stave of the riverbank,
Where even in our rapture we were shy.
A song yanked at our mouths like a bit.
Stampeding, we embraced its roan beat.

Accelerato, adagio—our soul
vacillating, forever wondering
what movement or coda might make the whole
emerge as that resolute rendering.
Welcoming transformations—staccato,
legato—all the while probing dreams
dreamed in the depths of our mind and heart,
curious—Are we ending . . . where to start?

We said things like, "That's some beautiful land,"
Before we dreamed we were awake. We said,
"Caves are rhetorical questions about lost hands."
"Descent is the last good word," we chanted.
Up the road, an ice cream truck played canned
Music. Its shrill sweetness went to our heads.
Ants gravitated to the melting song.
We trailed after them. We could not go wrong.

To inspire our last stanza, let's consider W.S. Merwin's 2005 *New &
Selected Poems*. The collection is called *Migration* because, Merwin told

the poet Tom Holmes, "each of us is alone" on our journey. Here are the final eight lines of Merwin's poem "Passing":

the telephone it was my father on his
own journey asking me to be surprised
not taking in a word about the house but asking
about changing money about where I could meet him
about trains for the Holy Land and when I drove him
from the station a long way through country he was seeing
for the first time he seemed to be seeing nothing
and I could not see it was the only time

I am glad for our communal poetic migration, and I very much look forward to reading the entries for the culmination of our canto. We'll cleave, of course, to Byron's rules: eight lines of (flexible) iambic pentameter, rhymed *abababcc*. This week's deadline is Saturday, August 22, midnight eastern time.

Humbling Back

August 25, 2015

Of the several fine stanzas submitted to close our canto, I chose Berwyn Moore's:

But now you humble back, the music lost
along the bank, the horses chuffing clouds,
caves quiet. Your gypsy soul sighs almost,
almost—but we all descend, don't we, cowed
by hunger, thinning hair, and years varicosed
with backfired plans. Let's rest, let's disavow
our pockets of bone, voices from the past.
Let's sink into our own delight at last.

Moore's stanza deftly echoes and intertwines motifs from throughout our canto. In a footnote, she credits W. B. Yeats, and her stanza's dramatization of how human frailty can engender wisdom is indeed Yeatsian—as demonstrated by Yeats's own "Men Improve with the Years," that begins: "I am worn out with dreams" and ends this way:

Delighted to be but wise,
For men improve with the years;
And yet, and yet,
Is this my dream, or the truth?
O would that we had met
When I had my burning youth!
But I grow old among dreams,
A weather-worn, marble triton
Among the streams.

In its "almost, / almost," Moore's stanza shares Yeats's lament for the energy of youth—and the realization that his dreams rest with him, permanent though worn. Moore's gift for images: the "horses chuffing clouds," her deft transformation of noun to verb: "years varicosed / with backfired plans" fuse body and soul, leading to triumphant rest. Resignation turns to hard-won happiness.

Second place is a three-way tie among stanzas by Jordan Sanderson, Charise Hoge, and Patricia Smith. Here is Sanderson's:

The sun did its rising while we packed.
We needed to get on the road, but it
Would not have us. The bees were distracted.
We tried to dress, but our clothes did not fit.
Honey combed our mouths, kept us off track.
The directions were lost in a postscript.
By the river we found a saxophone.
Inside it were new bodies, a new home.

The closing image is astonishing in the way it returns all the strivings of the poem to what might well be judged its start: the instrument that voices genius music from an obscure interior.

Here is Charise Hoge's stanza:

A faded bloom deserts its host, descends
below; falsetto notes cascading there.
A praying mantis our lamenting rends
unnecessary. Restlessness of air
drops chatter crumbling trail around a bend
. . . where I am sleeping in a shelter. Bare
and seasoned feet will rest a thousand nights
off pavement sheets, by forte rise to write.

These lines voice our canto's notes of necessary and natural loss, gracefully reprising melodies: the "seasoned feet" that have renounced shoes, the "thousand nights" of ancient stories that redeem the future, the impetuous strength of art.

Smith's stanza serves as an eloquent farewell letter to our canto, now complete:

No one proclaimed, "Oh, the places you'll go!"
Come join our caravan of dreams, yes, do.
Find dimensions and spaces till now unknown.
There are fences to scale, grand vistas to view,
connections to craft—create them just so—
and cadenced stops to orchestrate too.
Our journey now over, must such good things end?
Our spirits elated as our stanzas blend.

Here is our canto, its provisional title made permanent:

Caravan of Dreams

The trip begins without a sign that's hung.
The mark may lie within your palm a line
a psychic knew before your time was sung.
She saw the span of dissonance: you pine
to scale a chart, depart where others clung;
refuse the map, forget reviews unkind.
My year of birth your cry of "Something Else!!!!"
A gypsy soul keeps nothing on the shelf.

Charise Hoge

Refuse the map. Forego the sturdy shoes.
Shrug off the ragged water of the past.
Your antipodal star riffs like the blues.
Step double-time across the bones and vast
landscapes of asphalt and stubble. He woos
you still, and waits, declares he'll be the last.
His words flutter like ashes in the wind.
For once, run away, free, undisciplined.

Berwyn Moore

The sky was appaloosa, the town paint.
The electric train plucked by, and the sky
Was bone, and the wind fluted through its flank.
We emerged like half-notes from a horn sighed
Onto the slick stave of the riverbank,

Where even in our rapture we were shy.
A song yanked at our mouths like a bit.
Stampeding, we embraced its roan beat.

Jordan Sanderson

Accelerato, adagio—our soul
vacillating, forever wondering
what movement or coda might make the whole
emerge as that resolute rendering.
Welcoming transformations—staccato,
legato—all the while probing dreams
dreamed in the depths of our mind and heart,
curious—Are we ending . . . where to start?

Patricia Smith

We said things like, "That's some beautiful land,"
Before we dreamed we were awake. We said,
"Caves are rhetorical questions about lost hands."
"Descent is the last good word," we chanted.
Up the road, an ice cream truck played canned
Music. Its shrill sweetness went to our heads.
Ants gravitated to the melting song.
We trailed after them. We could not go wrong.

Jordan Sanderson

But now you humble back, the music lost
along the bank, the horses chuffing clouds,
caves quiet. Your gypsy soul sighs almost,
almost—but we all descend, don't we, cowed
by hunger, thinning hair, and years varicosed
with backfired plans. Let's rest, let's disavow
our pockets of bone, voices from the past.
Let's sink into our own delight at last.

Berwyn Moore

Thank you, Lord Byron, for the enduring design that guided us. And thank you, poets, for banding together for our caravansary, in which (to quote one of Paul Michelsen's fine stanzas from this week) "the words that we heard flew away like birds, and the birds that we heard flew away like words."

For next week, let's try a briefer project, one that I call "poemization." Often we've seen a story or novel re-emerge as a film. What if the process were taken in an opposite direction, with prose compressed to poetry? In audience size, this might mean diminishment—but in audience quality, perhaps the opposite. I consider this activity principally a homage to the original and rightful author, but also an experiment in accelerating a narrative's trajectory. I've done this with (or to) a number of Anton Chekhov's stories (as translated by Constance Garnett). "The Lady with the Pet Dog" begins this way, broken into lines:

Once I'd seduced her, there was no hurry.
I cut a slice of watermelon, ate it deliberately.
Afterwards we walked on the esplanade,
her white dog trotting behind us.
The shore seemed dead. A single boat rocking
a sleepy light, the sea's muffled sound,
monotonous.

What begins as casual summer seduction becomes something much larger, outfacing and supplanting the speaker's home life—his wife and son—and driving him toward the woman whom he now recognizes as no mere distraction but his one true love. He travels to the woman's town, tracks her to an opera house. Here are my version's last two stanzas:

At intermission Anna's husband went out
and I approached, said "Good Evening."
She sat staring—I stood, afraid
to sit down beside her. Together we jumped
at the blast a horn made tuning up. She rose
and hurried toward an exit. I followed, past
chests wearing badges, racks of jumbled
fur coats, the smell of stale
tobacco, a dozen bored conversations.
At the last place in the world, the entrance
to a narrow, gloomy staircase, she stopped
and we kissed, like man and wife,
like tender friends.

This is how we found ourselves in love
with no escape, the end still far
from our reach.

(The entire poem can be found in my collection, *Possession*, published by Red Hen.)

For next week, I propose that you "poemize" (or begin to poemize) a novel or short story. Do this in twenty lines or less, in verse formal or free or somewhere in between. Be sure to identify the text that you are working from. Submit your efforts no later than midnight eastern time on Saturday, August 29.

Snake-Eye

September 1, 2015

This week's first-place honors go to Patricia Smith's deft "poemization" of O. Henry's "The Ransom of Red Chief":

Bill and I hatched a plan
to finance our upcoming land scam in Illinois:
kidnap ten-year-old, red-haired son of
Ebenezer Dorset, Summit, Alabama.
Dorset to pay $2,000 ransom.

We snatched the kid, took him to our hideout.
Turns out he's a holy terror and loves our hideout.
Calls himself "Red Chief."
Christens Bill "Old Hank, the Trapper"
and me "Snake-eye, the Spy."
Threatens us with scalping and broiling.

Our plan backfires when old Dorset
demands $250 before he'll take his son back.
Bill and I finally drag Red Chief, kicking and screaming, back home,
pay the old man his $250 and take off running
before the kid can escape his father's ten-minute grip.

The lines are subtly linked with partial, often internal rhymes: "Ransom" aptly recalls "scam." As the stated plan goes awry, the final stanza loses composure, and the tenuous rhyme of "grip" with "Dorset" holds on just long enough for discomfort: a masterful job. For an entertaining film version, let me recommend 1952's O. Henry's *Full House*, directed by Henry Hathaway and Howard Hawks.

In second place, we have one of Paul Michelsen's several fine efforts. This one "poemizes" Flannery O'Connor's "A Good Man Is Hard to Find":

The Tennessee Waltz

Cotton field graveyard for half a dozen awaiting resurrection.
Children ignore the dead with their heads in the clouds.
Cows and cars crash in the sky and it rains blood, oil, and milk

At Red Sammy's diner, Mom paid a dime to play "The Tennessee Waltz"
"You can't win," Red Sammy said. And if the future proved him right
they wouldn't be a tall surprised. And Red Sammy also said this:
A good man is hard to find.

They'd seen it all wrong. It wasn't a cow, but a cat made the car roll over,
And it wasn't milk fell from the sky, but a cat o' nine tails made of
Snow-white pleather that God dropped, butterfingers that He sometimes is.

Behold, the easier kind of man to find, The Misfit—Grandmother prayed away,
or told everyone else to, anyway—Pray, pray, pray, she said—her way of trying to
keep the worst from taking place. Empty words as if a cat walked across
the keys on a toy piano. Say it like you mean it next time, if a next time ever
    comes.

Sidekicks escorted the family into the woods while The Misfit
stayed put with grandmother whose hair looked like clouds.

They had a talk. She had, oh, about sixty words or so left to say
It was as though the last few bit him hard
And then he left her sitting like a child looking up
Smiling at the big blank sky.

There is much to admire: for example, the astonishing second line, with its children ignoring "the dead with their heads in the clouds," and its echoing image of the grandmother, "sitting like a child looking up / Smiling at the big blank sky"; the surprisingly perfect image of the "cat o' nine tails made of / Snow-white pleather that God dropped butterfingers that He sometimes is," and the cat walking "across / the keys on a toy piano." Don't cats often do this, the piano invisible?

For next week, let's try writing a "hand of lies." Kenneth Koch, in his groundbreaking book on teaching poetry to children, *Wishes, Lies, and Dreams*, has the brilliant notion of not only allowing lies but encouraging them. Our new poems will tell five lines of lies, giving them syllable counts as follows:

Line one: seven syllables
Line two: nine syllables
Line three: eleven syllables
Line four: nine syllables
Line five: seven syllables

The hope is that the rigor of syllabics and the resultant shape will act as foil for our anarchy of untruths.

Submit your five-line stanzas no later than midnight eastern time on Saturday, September 5.

A Hand of Frightening Lies

September 8, 2015

This week's poets are wonderful prevaricators. Their skillful fibs create what Kenneth Koch might have called "fresh air." Out of several fine contenders, I choose Jordan Sanderson's:

The Roach

The roach did not speak to me.
It found my human form frightening.
It saw the kitchen light as a burning bush.
We did not share the tiramisu.
I did not kiss its dark wings.

    The required syllable count for our "hand of lies" (seven-nine-eleven-nine-seven) seems to encourage intensity in the longest line: "It saw the kitchen light as a burning bush." But the final line, returning to the initial syllable count, delivers an even deeper thrill. Sanderson's poem succeeds in appalling us with each implied reversal in this perverse encounter. The choice of "human form" is genius. Indeed, we are cut from the same cloth as the roach, a recognition sealed with the final kiss.

    In second place, we have Charise Hoge's hand of lies:

Falsity

Swift she got under his thumb,
wooed to wed, cooed to wife, taut by grip
of charm to shush the alarm of her senses.
She pivots from the apparition:
a suave glove knuckling contempt.

The Italian writer Elena Ferrante, whose Neopolitan quartet of novels have been discussed in *The American Scholar,* might well admire how Hoge's lies enact the contortion of self that certain men can inspire in vulnerable women—particularly within the traditional milieu that is Ferrante's context. Sheltered by falsity, such women have a cruel choice: escape or permanent effacement. Hoge's brief poem dexterously employs hands—their physical, symbolic, and metonymic power—to deliver "Falsity" a knock-out blow.

This week I would like to inaugurate a new prize category, "Funniest Poem." Hands down, this honor goes to Paul Michelsen's darkly hilarious entry:

One Hiccup in an Otherwise Perfect Evening

A magician once made me
vanish. Her name was Elizabeth.
There's only one problem with what Lizzie did
(I was told her last name was Boredom):
She brought me back cut in half.

For this week, we'll reprise one of David Lehman's genius prompts, a group cento, but forge it from distinct material. Let's call it "Cento Resartus." I'd like you to write a four-line stanza, in flexible iambic pentameter, rhymed or unrhymed, using language (think phrase or sentence rather than individual words) from Thomas Carlyle's 1836 novel, said to foreshadow postmodernism, *Sartor Resartus.* (It is widely available online.)

I do not recommend that you read (or reread) the entire work. The idea is to "poemize" Carlyle's phrasing into a lively, arresting, perhaps mysterious stanza. Swift rather than labored composition might work best. We will create a group-composed cento of up to four stanzas. No title is needed at this point. Have fun, and remember to submit your stanza no later than midnight eastern time, Saturday, September 12.

Philosophy of Clothes

September 15, 2015

How inspiring to read this week's repurposing of Carlyle's language and to witness his "flesh-garment of language" worn by new imaginations. No "show-cloaks," no specious constructions here! Our "Cento Resartus" will begin with Patricia Smith's beautifully made stanza:

With what shall this Philosophy of Clothes
clothe its naked Truth—rough woolen cloak
of the countryside or silken mantle—
obscuring yet exposing its muscle, its os?

Smith's commanding question seems an apt beginning for a dialogue between the tangible and invisible, the outward and inward selves. "Clothes" and "os," felicitously linked by rhyme, form a rich contradiction to carry us forward.

In second place, we have this intriguing stanza tailored by Paul Michelsen:

Tissue glories in its Lawrences
forsaking gold-mines of finance and slaughter
Clothed with Beauty and with Curses
safe-moored in some still obscurity

In these lines, Carlyle seems to wear the passions of romanticism's William Blake, as well as those of the great twentieth-century proponent of the body, D.H. Lawrence. In the phrase, "forsaking gold-mines of finance and slaughter," we are reminded that Carlyle named economics "The Dismal Science."

Honorable mention goes to Jan Nielsen's sexy and spiritual entry:

Yet all was tight and right there: hot and black
in minute incessant fluctuation
to get in motion, and seemed crank and slack
"the very Spirit of Love embodied"

Cento-making retailors language wholesale, fashioning thought in a way consonant with Carlyle's desire that society transcend itself in new lexicons, fresh expressions of the soul.

Next week's challenge is to fashion a second stanza to shape our poetic garment. Again using phrases from Thomas Carlyle's *Sartor Resartus*, stitch four lines of approximate iambic pentameter, rhymed or unrhymed. Remember to submit your efforts no later than midnight, eastern time, on Saturday, September 19.

Clothwebs and Cobwebs

September 22, 2015

Poets, thank you for this week's entries. I was tempted by all but chose Berwyn Moore's stanza as most fitting:

Society . . . is founded upon cloth,
clothwebs and cobwebs, dead fleeces of sheep.
Logic-choppers stupidly grope about.
Hunger-bitten, they kiss your pudding-cheek.

Moore's selection of "clothwebs and cobwebs" reminds us of the transience of fashion, its ability to numb and mummify, and its propensity to insulate the rich from the distress of others. "Dead fleeces of sheep" imply their opposite, the legendary golden fleece sought by Jason. The send-up of "logic-choppers" is both comical and expressive of the spirit of Carlyle, especially the slightly creepy "pudding-cheek."

In second place we have Paul Michelsen's haunting arrangement:

Visible and tangible products of the Past, again, I reckon
in this solemn moment comes a man, or monster, scrambling
Not like a dead city of stones, yearly crumbling
this paltry little Dog-cage of an Earth.

In his prophetic rendering of Carlyle, Michelsen makes the very Earth both garment and prison.

Our third-place stanza is Jordan Sanderson's:

Work of genius like the very Sun has
Black spots and troubled nebulosities.
Tailoring, man proceeds by Accident.
We hope we are strangers to all the world.

Vladimir Mayakovsky's 1914 poem styles him "A Cloud in Trousers." Perhaps most of us more resemble Carlyle and Sanderson's "troubled nebulosities," tailors proceeding "by Accident," and sometimes creating beauty.

Indeed, we find lovely moments in each contributed stanza. Who could ignore LaWanda Walters's genius selection of "pursy chuckle"; or Paul Michelsen's discovery of "red streaks of unspeakable grandeur"; or, for that matter, Patricia Smith's choice find, "free flight of vestural Thought?"

Our cento so far reads as follows:

With what shall this Philosophy of Clothes
clothe its naked Truth—rough woolen cloak
of the countryside or silken mantle—
obscuring yet exposing its muscle, its os?   *Patricia Smith*

Society . . . is founded upon cloth,
clothwebs and cobwebs, dead fleeces of sheep.
Logic-choppers stupidly grope about.
Hunger-bitten, they kiss your pudding-cheek.   *Berwyn Moore*

To lead into next week's prompt, here is a brief poem from my first book (published by Owl Creek Press) *Kneeling Between Parked Cars.*

Learning to Sew

Crossing my legs in front of you, I am
your tailor.

I will make you a suit.
What size? The size of a tree
coming into its own.

A jacket with elbow room
for a small stream.

And what shall I use for a pattern?
The Mississippi River Basin.

You will wear this suit
only to the big occasions.

To the building
of anthills,

to the opening
of a door.

Don't look,
here it is now,

shouldering its way
into the room.

Next week will unveil our ending: we are designing a three-piece cento. The rules have altered. For our finale, I'd like you to use any published writing on fashion. Any genre is fair game. You may mash your found language with Carlyle's *Sartor Resartus* or leave Carlyle out—your choice. The only rule for the stanza is that it must contain four lines. In other words, you may forget (or keep) iambic pentameter. You may also employ your own wording for transitions, or for other relatively small purposes. We are redesigning our garment, making it more fluid. I hope you will enjoy brainstorming just what might constitute a perfect fit. Remember to credit your source(s), and to submit your efforts no later than midnight eastern time on Saturday, September 26.

Three-Piece Cento with Extra Pants

September 29, 2015

What genius tailoring in this week's cento entries. Let's take Paul Michelsen's suggestion—slightly altered—for the title. I choose one of his stanzas as our waistcoat—a snazzy one indeed:

There is no arguing with the fashion.
Interpreters of that same holy mystery
wait to make the proper drop-dead entrance
in torched and tumbled chiffon.

    Sources:
Folkways by William Graham Sumner
Sartor Resartus by Thomas Carlyle
Tom Wolfe's introduction to *A La Mode: On the Social Psychology of Fashion* by
    René König
"Couture" by Mark Doty

    Michelsen's materials come together in a wryly humorous, elegant stanza, stitching satire to beauty.
    And for our extra trousers, since, as we know well, they wear out first, I choose Berwyn Moore's durable weave:

Let the wench pull a garment from its hanger
like she's choosing a body and wear it like skin.
Let us thatch ourselves anew. Let be be finale of seam.
Thus does the good Homer not only nod, but snore.

    Sources:
"The Emperor of Ice-Cream" by Wallace Stevens (She changed "seem" to
    "seam.")

"What Do Women Want?" by Kim Addonizio
Sartor Resartus by Thomas Carlyle

Carlyle himself would appreciate Moore's punning "seam." And how perfect to end with the great blind poet, who knew fashion by touch alone, yet wove world-making stories, and *Sartor Resartus*, the work that threaded our poetic needles.

There is much more that deserves mention: how stunning Patricia Smith's selection of Yeats's ". . . a tress Of dull red hair . . . flowing Over some silken dress . . . ." And how delightful to be invited to LaWanda Walters's 1970s swimming hole, and to view her collision of Thomas Carlyle and David Byrne. I agree with Paul Michelsen's comment on our cento: "It's a strange and exhilarating way of collaborating with both the living and the dead."

Now it's time to remove our thimbles and leave the untouched bolts of poetry for future garments.

Three-Piece Cento with Extra Pants

With what shall this Philosophy of Clothes
clothe its naked Truth—rough woolen cloak
of the countryside or silken mantle—
obscuring yet exposing its muscle, its os?   *Patricia Smith*

Society . . . is founded upon cloth,
clothwebs and cobwebs, dead fleeces of sheep.
Logic-choppers stupidly grope about.
Hunger-bitten, they kiss your pudding-cheek.   *Berwyn Moore*

There is no arguing with the fashion.
Interpreters of that same holy mystery
wait to make the proper drop-dead entrance
in torched and tumbled chiffon.   *Paul Michelsen*

Let the wench pull a garment from its hanger
like she's choosing a body and wear it like skin.
Let us thatch ourselves anew. Let be be finale of seam.
Thus does the good Homer not only nod, but snore.   *Berwyn Moore*

I am thrilled to announce next Tuesday's return of quizmaster David Lehman, fresh from the launch of the brand-new *Best American Poetry*, and with his *Sinatra's Century: One Hundred Notes on the Man and His World* excitingly close to its publication date. In his poem "January 10," David responds to the question, "How was your fall?" with "I'm still falling." I can't wait for David to make us fall for poetry in ways as yet unimagined. We can guess that his new prompts will be, as always, exacting but not pedantic, and with his special flair: a twist appearing like a je-ne-sais-quoi shadow from a city doorway.

Thank you, generous poets, for taking part in our summer's experiments in verse. Your enthusiasm for the tasks set before you has buoyed me more than you can guess, and your every kind comment was received and appreciated.

And so, good-bye for now. I'm glad to say that I may have other chances to task you with poetry; should David again need a designated hitter for "Next Line, Please," I will be ready.

Let's Do It Again

A New Crowd-Sourced Sonnet, One Line at a Time

By David Lehman

October 6, 2015

I'm glad to be back at the helm of "Next Line, Please." I needed the three-month hiatus and am very grateful to Angela Ball for the excellent job she did running the competitions in my absence.

We began this column in May 2014 with the sonnet as our rite of initiation. We set out to test the notion that we could build one collaboratively, line by line; for speed and diversity, we would capitalize on the capability of advanced electronics. Over the course of fifteen weeks, we composed a collective sonnet, in rhyme, entitled "Monday." I propose that we kick off the fall season by competing for the best first line of a new crowd-sourced sonnet. There is only one requirement: The line must end with the word "uniform," preferably with a comma following it. *C'est tout.*

Remember that the modern sonneteer enjoys freedoms unknown to Renaissance or romantic poets. So let's agree that our sonnet should consist of fourteen lines, with the last word of each line specified by the quizmaster. We need not comply with a regular metrical scheme except perhaps to the extent that the phrase—whether in the musical or linguistic sense—tends toward a loose iambic with strategic deviations into dactyls, anapests, trochees, and spondees. Let me worry about it.

I am certain that contestants can do better than the first line that occurred to me after settling on "uniform" as our end word: "The tree camouflaged in its green uniform."

Deadline: midnight, Saturday, October 10. Good luck to all. It's good to be back.

Uniformity

October 13, 2015

There were so many good entries this week that it was even harder than usual to pick out a winner. I went with Michael C. Rush's entry: "Our dreams as disparate as our days uniform," in part because I think we can do interesting things with the antithesis set up between night and day, dreams and actuality. There is an implicit "are" between "days" and "uniform." But I was also intrigued by the possibility of an invisible apostrophe after "days." That is, a listener without seeing the poem might think that the word uniform in "days['] uniform" refers to an item of apparel. It is clear that the primary meaning has to do with sameness (uniformity), but the buried metaphor has a definite appeal.

Second place goes to Charise Hoge for "A new tattoo, another tour in uniform," for the concreteness of the image and the timely reminder that we have troops abroad.

For third place, I liked both Lauren MacArthur's "A thread—the length of a bullet—defiled her uniform" and Karen Topham's "Each, right hand over heart, exactly five squares apart, stood uniform." MacArthur's choice of verb won me over as did Topham's brilliant internal rhyme of "heart" and "apart."

Honorable mention to John Tranter ("Sonnets all have fourteen lines, they're uniform") for reminding us that there is a tradition of sonnets about the sonnet form (Wordsworth, Keats) and Patricia Smith ("Words, like soldiers waiting in uniform"), who introduces a potent simile that we could easily elaborate.

On a TV series recently, a character reporting to his boss summarizes his advice, pauses, and concludes: "I could be wrong." The boss replies, "How many times have you said that and meant it?" It was an excellent exchange, and it made its point efficiently. But when I say "I could be wrong" in this context, I mean it. That's just an acknowledgment of the frank subjectivity that enters into a competition—or an editorial process.

For next week, we will write line two of our crowd-sourced sonnet. The only rule is that the line must end with either "known" or "well known" followed by either a semicolon or a period.

Deadline: Sunday, October 18 at noon (any U.S. time zone). Good luck, and thank you.

Wouldn't It Be Loverly?

October 20, 2015

The many strong contenders for line two of our sonnet could pull our work-in-progress in as many different directions. The candidate that I liked the most, which points to the direction that strikes me as most promising, is Angela Ball's "We crave a lovely scandal with someone well-known." After our strong opening line, with its abstract formulation, how refreshing to modulate to something as concrete and ever-timely as a "lovely scandal." The phrase is almost an oxymoron, but its plain sense will be lost on no one. Everything from old-fashioned tabloids to the latest in social media reminds us that we're hooked on scandals. We can't get enough of them—whether it's a case of financial malfeasance on a colossal scale, a spymaster caught pants down with a fetching enemy agent, a celebrated actress caught shoplifting, or dozens of variants. We are suckers for such stories—to the point that it might be said that we "crave" them. But Angela's choice of "crave" has an extra effect, implying that the spectator may harbor a secret wish to be a player—rather than an observer or bystander—in just such a scandal.

Second-place honors go to Charise Hoge for "What secrets pitch their tents on borders known?" It is a muscular line of strong, assertive iambic pentameter, and it is tempting to pick up the baton where the line leaves off, with "secrets" and "borders."

Though I don't fully understand it, MQ's entry, "We walk the sheets until the bell, well known," captivated me. I was baffled by the first phrase, though "walk the sheets" sounds enough like "walk the streets" to make this a nonproblem. And it would be a pleasure to imagine the bodies in, or the sentences or musical phrases written on, these ghostly "sheets"—which are visible perhaps only until the "bell" signifying day-break sounds.

Honorable mentions: LaWanda Walters ("rearrange the yesterday we thought we had known"), Brian Tholl ("The oneiric craftsman lies masked among the known"), and Elizabeth Solsburg ("We rifle through them for truths we've known").

So here we are:

Our dreams as disparate as our days uniform,
We crave a lovely scandal with someone well-known;

Line three needs to end with the word "thunderstorm," preferably followed by a comma.

Deadline: Sunday, October 25, at noon. My sincere thanks to all who took part. Please know that I read your line—I read every line—at least thrice, and usually more.

Midnight Champagne

October 27, 2015

These were my five finalists for line three of our sonnet in progress:

To make love in the aura of a thunderstorm, (Angela Ball)
Come id, unbidden rain, thwarted thunderstorm (Joe Lawlor)
First hot, quick lightning. Then [a] dark, deep thunderstorm (Joanna Peders)
Midnight champagne, penthouse lit by thunderstorm, (Christine Rhein)
Spotlit by the lightning of a media thunderstorm, (Elizabeth Solsburg)

I was almost tempted to put it to a general vote but decided not to pass the buck. After hemming and hawing, I opted for Christine Rhein's line "Midnight champagne, penthouse lit by thunderstorm." I like the way the "lovely scandal" of line two turns luxurious ("penthouse") but with tremors of danger ("lit by thunderstorm"). It is a very cinematic line, and the bubbly at the stroke of midnight means either that it is New Year's Eve or that there is something gothic in the movie that we're in.

In their differing ways Angela Ball's line and Joanna Peders's line elaborate our poem in desirable directions: Angela's to a level of romantic intimacy, Joanna's to a place where the weather is entirely metaphorical and erotic. Elizabeth Solsburg introduces the media into the equation, while Joe Lawlor turns to Freud, the id, and the repression of wishes expressed as meteorological conditions.

To all five, my compliments. Our sonnet is in good hands. Here it is so far:

Our dreams as disparate as our days uniform,
We crave a lovely scandal with someone well-known;
Midnight champagne, penthouse lit by thunderstorm,

Now we need to complete the first rhymed quatrain of our poem. The only requirement for next week is this:
The last word of our next line must be *alone.*

Darkness Visible

November 3, 2015

The requirement for this week's line—line four of our opening quatrain—is that it end with the word "alone." It is also understood that the line needs to follow our first three lines, and it has an added burden: it must create a sense of temporary closure. A heterodox line might work, but most of the fourteen finalists opted to aim at a stanza-ending line that introduces an element that we may want to develop in our next stanza.

To recapitulate, these are our first three lines, each with the name of its author:

Our dreams as disparate as our days uniform,   *Michael C. Rush*
We crave a lovely scandal with someone well-known;   *Angela Ball*
Midnight champagne, penthouse lit by thunderstorm,   *Christine Rhein*

For line four I chose Elizabeth Solsburg's:

In this version of darkness, we are never alone.

What I particularly liked was "this version of darkness." What, then, is darkness? If it is absence of light, how can it coexist with the lightning that sparks a thunderstorm? There is, of course, a metaphorical sense of darkness that Ms. Solsburg's line taps into. But look, too, at the possibilities raised by the alliteration of "darkness" with "dreams," "disparate," and "days" from line one; by the paradox of being plural ("we") yet "alone"; and by the recognition that this is just one "version" of a story. There may well be others.

In second place, running neck and neck with the winner, and falling behind by a nose, is Joanna Peders's:

Outside a city full, inside I sit with one glass, alone.

In addition to this line's other virtues, the antithesis between outside and inside seems an echo of the one between night and day in line one. Now, too, we have the emergence of an "I" to modify the stately "we" we had been working with. And "alone" picks up "one" as the line slams shut. Has reality interrupted the fantasy of line three, itself suggested by the tabloid news story in line two?

For third place, I lean to Paul Michelsen for "Instead of fridge-lit sour milk insomnia faced alone," though I also appreciated a second entry that Paul submitted: "In the morning woke—broke, naked, alone." It is beyond dispute that "fridge-lit sour milk insomnia" will stop any reader in her or his tracks.

Honorable mention: Joe Lawlor ("Still we have each other, together, alone."), Berwyn Moore ("Satin sheets, piano keys—we pretend we're alone."), Charise Hoge ("Clinking of glass . . . blackout, shattered, alone."), Terry Blackhawk ("An elaborate ruse so we don't dream alone."), and Kerry Hentges ("But instead we wake up, sheets tangled, alone.")

So here is our first stanza:

Our dreams as disparate as our days uniform,
We crave a lovely scandal with someone well-known;
Midnight champagne, penthouse lit by thunderstorm,
In this version of darkness, we are never alone.

For the opening line of our second quatrain, line five of our poem, I am looking for a line that ends with either "he" or "she," and preferably in the locution "but she" or "but he."

Good luck! Deadline: noon, Sunday, November 8.

Caged but Free . . .

November 10, 2015

Line five of our sonnet in progress is also the first line of our second stanza. A lot rides on it. The best candidate, in my view, is Christine Rhein's "If marriage is a cage, we can force the lock, but he . . ." This line introduces the subject of marriage, the metaphor of the locked cage, and the conditional construction that leaves the reader wondering what "he" will do and how that will affect our situation of dreams, scandal, penthouse, and darkness lit up by lightning.

Second place goes to Millicent Caliban's "She, embraced by a god invisible, but he." I confess to stumbling a bit over the absent verb in the first part of the line. But I am charmed by the image of "a god invisible," and I hope Millicent will continue to propose lines.

I would award third place to Vicki Peterson for "Left hand gold glimmers; we remove it, but she." Again there is the subject of marriage, but here we have the wedding band and the mysteriousness of a collective effort to remove it from the lady's ring finger.

Honorable mention: Angela Ball, with her clever allusion to John Berryman's dream songs ("The man of my dreams was my toy, my rest, but he").

For line six—the second line of stanza two of our sonnet in the making—the requirement is that the line must end with the word "learn." Yes, I have something up my sleeve, but I won't reveal what it is until later . . .

Here's where we are now:

Our dreams as disparate as our days uniform,	*Michael C. Rush*
We crave a lovely scandal with someone well-known;	*Angela Ball*
Midnight champagne, penthouse lit by thunderstorm,	*Christine Rhein*
In this version of darkness, we are never alone.	*Elizabeth Solsburg*
If marriage is a cage, we can force the lock, but he	*Christine Rhein*

Deadline: noon on Sunday, November 15.

The Key That Confirms the Lock

November 17, 2015

There were four finalists for this week's winning entry. Here they are:

If marriage is a cage, we can force the lock, but he
clutches the key, a jailer too stubborn to learn
Patricia Smith

If marriage is a cage, we can force the lock, but he
is not a dove. He is a hawk and hawks can learn
Helen P.

If marriage is a cage, we can force the lock, but he
forgot where the getaway car is parked. He'll never learn
Paul Michelsen

If marriage is a cage, we can force the lock, but he
Who thinks marriage a cage will soon learn
Michael C. Rush

I love Michael C. Rush's unexpected repetition of the "if" clause of the previous line. Paul Michelsen's line is funny and charming and conducts us with fabulous swiftness from the metaphor of the locked cage to the realm of cops and robbers and getaway cars. An excellent example of iambic hexameter, Helen's line keeps the cage and adds the birds—doves and hawks, birds that we have, since at least the time of the Vietnam War, charged with political significance. Patricia Smith adds the key, the jailer (who may well be our protagonist), and the possibility that the jailer may be a prisoner in disguise.

Well, any of the four would serve us well, but that's not a practical solution, so I'll make the tough call. I pick Patricia Smith for first prize, Paul Michelsen for first runner-up, Helen P. for second runner-up, and Michael C. Rush for honorable mention.

Our next line—line three of stanza two—must end with "turn" or "to turn" as we complete an *abba* stanza, the rhymed stanza that

Tennyson used with perfection in "In Memoriam." Note the average length of our lines and try to follow suit. Bear in mind that "learn" here can be intransitive—i.e., it does not need an object—or transitive. So our next line can specify what it is that he "learns," or it can assume that line six has come to a full end. Either "too stubborn to learn / how to sit still for sixty minutes and then turn" or "too stubborn to learn / and too proud to stand up, back off, and turn" would work, to offer two examples that come to mind.

Here's where we are now:

Our dreams as disparate as our days uniform,	*Michael C. Rush*
We crave a lovely scandal with someone well-known;	*Angela Ball*
Midnight champagne, penthouse lit by thunderstorm,	*Christine Rhein*
In this version of darkness, we are never alone.	*Elizabeth Solsburg*
If marriage is a cage, we can force the lock, but he	*Christine Rhein*
Clutches the key, a jailer too stubborn to learn	*Patricia Smith*

Deadline: Sunday, November 22, at noon.

Are the Words of the Prophets Written on Prison Walls?

November 24, 2015

Paul Michelsen, a stalwart contributor to these contests, has submitted two fine possibilities for line seven: "To read the graffiti. If need be, he can turn" and "Just what these clues mean—perhaps he will turn." Both fit the context; both demonstrate the value of a caesura, and both serve well as transitional lines. Whichever is chosen needs to be completed in line eight, the stanza's ultimate line.

I will go with the first of these, liking the way the line plays against an iambic base. Arguably the most important moment in the line is "the graffiti," a sentence-ending phrase that substitutes a dactyl for an iamb and leaves us with the mystery of a text message: what does the graffiti say?

There's a three-way tie for second-place honors: Charise Hoge's "There's a mirror wherever he may turn" puts us in a fun house, as in the thrilling climax of Orson Welles's movie *The Lady from Shanghai* in which Rita Hayworth and Everett Sloan shoot at each other's images.

Millicent Caliban (who someday will disclose how she or he came up with that moniker) offers the deliberately poetical hexameter: "That hope with feathery wing from tyrant's clutch will turn"—a nod to Emily Dickinson's depiction of "hope" and a strategic inversion of regular word order ("from tyrant's clutch will turn").

Berwyn Moore gets kudos for her robust line of strong iambic pentameter: "The span of sigh and touch, turn and counter-turn." The last part of that line recalls the patterns of Roman odes—such as Ben Jonson's Pindaric ode "To the Immortal Memory and Friendship of That Noble Pair, Sir Lucius Cary and Sir Henry Morison."

Honorable mention goes to Byron for the effort to relate our sonnet to recent events ("The fate of fanatics in St. Denis who turn") and J. F. McCullers for the elegant balancing act that is "Too proud to plead, and ever too loyal to turn."

Here, then, is where we are:

Our dreams as disparate as our days uniform,	*Michael C. Rush*
We crave a lovely scandal with someone well-known;	*Angela Ball*
Midnight champagne, penthouse lit by thunderstorm,	*Christine Rhein*
In this version of darkness, we are never alone.	*Elizabeth Solsburg*
If marriage is a cage, we can force the lock, but he	*Christine Rhein*
Clutches the key, a jailer too stubborn to learn	*Patricia Smith*
To read the graffiti. If need be, he can turn	*Paul Michelsen*

Our next line must end with the word *be* or the words *to be.*
Deadline: noon, Sunday November 29.
Thanks, everyone.

From Bouquet to Wreath

December 1, 2015

The task this week was to write line eight of our poem in progress—the last line of the second stanza as we near the point at which the sonnet shall pivot. The requirement was to end with "be" or "to be," thus rhyming the new line with line five. Faced with these lines,

> If marriage is a cage, we can force the lock, but he
> Clutches the key, a jailer too stubborn to learn
> To read the graffiti. If need be, he can turn

the writer who goes by the name "Poem Today" came up with the winning entry:

> A bouquet to a wreath. Then we will be

Thanks to the author of line eight, our poem has complicated its base of imagery from cage, lock, jailer, and key. We now have flowers—the symbol of beauty and innocence that marks occasions as happy as nuptials and as fatal as funerals. Has the ceremony of innocence come to grief, with these flowers left behind? The winning line has the virtue of suspending itself in mid-air, so our next six lines can take us on a journey far from the desolation implied in our intellectually rich second stanza.

Second-place honors this week go to Vicki Peterson for ending not with a whimper but a bang:

> To read the graffiti. If need be, he can turn
> The gun on himself, solve every problem and be

The sentence ends with a cliffhanger that would have been fun to resolve if it were possible to go in more than one direction at a time.

Third prize goes to the redoubtable Patricia Smith, who gives us

To read the graffiti. If need be, he can turn
Scry into the crystal, foresee what might be

The line contains the beautiful verb "scry," which—in its meaning of fortune-telling with a crystal ball—I recall encountering only once before: in T. S. Eliot's *Four Quartets*.

Honorable mention goes to Emily Sierra Poertner, who suggested

To read the graffiti. If need be, he can turn
Back into who he used to be.

The simplicity of the line is one of its strengths. It relies on monosyllables marking iambic time except for the leading trochee. This subtle balance of the colloquial and the regular is something Robert Frost excelled at. We could use more of it in contemporary poetry.

I got a kick, too, out of Byron's candidate,

To read the graffiti. If need be, he can turn
Out to be an actor reciting "to be or not to be."

Our next line must end with "must." I would regard it as a plus if the line clarified the identity of the character known as "he." Who is he? The husband? The dreamer? The cop on the beat? The vice president in charge of morale? The conductor? The governor? The hero? The hunted man? Alternatively: who are we?

Here's where we are so far:

Our dreams as disparate as our days uniform,   *Michael C. Rush*
We crave a lovely scandal with someone well-known;   *Angela Ball*
Midnight champagne, penthouse lit by thunderstorm,   *Christine Rhein*
In this version of darkness, we are never alone.   *Elizabeth Solsburg*

If marriage is a cage, we can force the lock, but he   *Christine Rhein*
Clutches the key, a jailer too stubborn to learn   *Patricia Smith*
To read the graffiti. If need be, he can turn   *Paul Michelsen*
A bouquet to a wreath. Then we will be   *Poem Today*

Deadline: Sunday, December 6, at noon.

Terms of Interment

December 8, 2015

Line nine of our sonnet needs to introduce the rhyme word "must." It also kicks off the last six lines in the poem. The previous line ended mid-sentence: "Then we will be."

To complete the sentence, I chose Angela Ball's

Two mourners arguing terms of interment. We must

I was persuaded by the alliteration (mourners, must) and wordplay ("terms of interment") and pleased, too, that the line ends with the appearance of a new subject and verb and a wide-open set of possibilities.

Runners-up: Dick Humbird's paradoxical "Compelled no more to suffer what we must" and Joanna Peders's "The silent marker on lovers' graves—we must."

I'd also like to mention most honorably Vicki Peterson's "loveless sans lover—you, buried alive, and I, must" and Berwyn Moore's "Lovers refusing to grieve or believe we must."

So here's where we are:

Our dreams as disparate as our days uniform,	*Michael C. Rush*
We crave a lovely scandal with someone well-known;	*Angela Ball*
Midnight champagne, penthouse lit by thunderstorm,	*Christine Rhein*
In this version of darkness, we are never alone.	*Elizabeth Solsburg*

If marriage is a cage, we can force the lock, but he	*Christine Rhein*
Clutches the key, a jailer too stubborn to learn	*Patricia Smith*

To read the graffiti. If need be, he can turn   *Paul Michelsen*
A bouquet to a wreath. Then we will be   *Poem Today*

Two mourners arguing terms of interment. We must   *Angela Ball*

What we need now is line ten. It must complete the sentence, preferably in a way that blends surprise and vigor. The requirement: the line must end with the words "subject to."

Good luck, everyone. Deadline: Sunday, December 13, noon.

Bliss Is Momentary in the Mind

December 15, 2015

For line ten I asked for a line that ended with the words "subject to."
I offered to propose a line or two, and people welcomed the intrusion.
I came up with

Two mourners arguing terms of interment. We must
Refuse; must fuse our forces; for love is only subject to

and

Two mourners arguing terms of interment. We
Refuse; must fuse our forces; for love is a tough subject to

I liked the idea of alternative senses of "subject to . . ." As a noun it leads
to "master"; as a subordinate phrase it leads to "the laws of" or "the rules
of." The opposite sides of the same motif.

Bewitched by the internal rhyme and heavy alliteration, I decided that
I would use the first of these lines, a fanfare for love, until and unless
something came along that made me change my mind. I was very taken
with Millicent Caliban's entry, so aphoristic, with an internal rhyme that
mimes the effect of a couplet by Alexander Pope:

Two mourners arguing terms of interment. We must
Hide from the common view what flesh is subject to

Then came three entries by Berwyn Moore. One in particular ap-
pealed to me:

Two mourners arguing terms of interment. We must
Appease our lust, our momentary bliss subject to

I went with Berwyn Moore's line because it maintains a high level of seriousness, reintroduces "lust" and "bliss" into our meditation, and allows for a continuation of the thought in the next line.

Other worthy lines were Elizabeth Solsburg's "We must / strike a match and burn the contract we are subject to" and Charisse Hoge's witty "We must / object [to] the loss of a subject." Paul Michelsen's wins honors for the week's funniest line, always a valuable distinction: "We must / Bury the rudest nudist we've ever been subject to."

So this is where we are:

Our dreams as disparate as our days uniform,	*Michael C. Rush*
We crave a lovely scandal with someone well-known;	*Angela Ball*
Midnight champagne, penthouse lit by thunderstorm,	*Christine Rhein*
In this version of darkness, we are never alone.	*Elizabeth Solsburg*

If marriage is a cage, we can force the lock, but he	*Christine Rhein*
Clutches the key, a jailer too stubborn to learn	*Patricia Smith*
To read the graffiti. If need be, he can turn	*Paul Michelsen*
A bouquet to a wreath. Then we will be	*Poem Today*

Two mourners arguing terms of interment. We must	*Angela Ball*
Appease our lust, our momentary bliss subject to	*Berwyn Moore*

Our next line should be looked at as both the eleventh line of the sonnet and the line that completes this three-line stanza. Your line must end with the word "just," whether lowercase or capitalized. The word "just" can be a noun ("the Last of the Just"), an adjective ("the just critic"), a synonym for "only" ("just kidding"), or part of a compound phrase ("just in time").

I keep hearing the phrase "the rules of engagement" on talk shows, and it would please me if your proposed line were to begin with this phrase, which has a military meaning but also a spousal one. But that is optional.

Deadline: noon, Sunday, December 19. Thanks, all.

The Rules of Engagement

December 22, 2015

For line eleven of our sonnet in progress, I was typically undecided until the last possible moment, when I went with Joe Lawlor's "The rules of engagement. The conflicts of lust. Just."

The third stanza of our poem is now complete, although syntactically unresolved.

Two mourners arguing terms of interment. We must
Appease our lust, our momentary bliss subject to
The rules of engagement. The conflicts of lust. Just

Though I have lopped off the period at the end of the stanza, you have the option of restoring it. After all, poets revise as they go, and writing a new line may make one want to alter, however subtly, an earlier line. It is all process, all journey, and the amount of minutiae rewards the control freak who likes seeing what language can do.

Joe Lawlor's line is a crisply delivered summary of the contradictions that energize our poem: do "rules of engagement" equal "conflict of lust"? Is it in the end lust rather than love that drives us from scandal to jail with a possible escape clause? Is that merely one hypothesis, or is it worth exploring the overlap between the military sense of the phrase and the amatory application we are making of it? Are we doomed to clash? If the word "Just" leaves us hanging at the edge of space, well, so much the better for the ingenious poet faced with the task of writing the next line.

Second prize goes to Charise Hoge's "Change, the clamor of amorous nights might just." The line follows its powerful opening syllable with a musicality difficult to resist: the rhymes of clamor and amorous, nights and might.

I thought highly of such other lines as Charise's second candidate, "The rules of engagement, the roll of the dice. Just"; Millicent Caliban's

"Rules of engagement not dreamt of by the just"; and Robert Stulberg's "The rules of engagement, which, though binding, are not just."

So this is where we are:

Our dreams as disparate as our days uniform,	*Michael C. Rush*
We crave a lovely scandal with someone well-known;	*Angela Ball*
Midnight champagne, penthouse lit by thunderstorm,	*Christine Rhein*
In this version of darkness, we are never alone.	*Elizabeth Solsburg*
If marriage is a cage, we can force the lock, but he	*Christine Rhein*
Clutches the key, a jailer too stubborn to learn	*Patricia Smith*
To read the graffiti. If need be, he can turn	*Paul Michelsen*
A bouquet to a wreath. Then we will be	*Poem Today*
Two mourners arguing terms of interment. We must	*Angela Ball*
Appease our lust, our momentary bliss subject to	*Berwyn Moore*
The rules of engagement. The conflicts of lust. Just	*Joe Lawlor*

The next line (line twelve) must end with the word "too" rhyming with line ten. It will serve as the opening line of the sonnet's concluding three-line stanza.

Deadline: Sunday, December 27 at noon.

Looking Ahead

December 29, 2015

Line twelve of our sonnet must end with "too," and we had no short-age of variant uses of that word. I was charmed by many but decided on these five finalists. In each case I include the previous line and retain the stanza break so you can see the immediate context (which is changed subtly in Robert Schultz's entry):

The rules of engagement. The conflicts of lust. Just
Look at the way they look at us. As though we're too
Brandon Crist

The rules of engagement. The conflicts of lust. Just
Pack your stuff; for me, infamy, maybe discharge too
Charise Hoge

The rules of engagement. The conflicts of lust. Just
Pour the drink! The way in is the way out, too.
Michael C. Rush

The rules of engagement. The conflicts of lust. "Just
Wait for the next wave," we tell ourselves, too
Robert Schultz

The rules of engagement. The conflicts of lust. Just
Step into the ring and circle each other until we are too
Elizabeth Solsburg

Let's take a closer look at this five-fingered exercise. Although each line is an imperative, you couldn't ask for more variety among the commanding verbs—*look, pack, pour, step,* and *wait.* It is almost as though we had found ourselves in a game—with each verb standing for a major life-changing decision. Robert Schultz transports us to the sea, Elizabeth Solsburg to the wrestling ring. Michael Rush proposes a sideways toast to Heraclitus (who said that the way up and the way down are the same). Charise Hoge packs a lot into her line: departure, infamy, discharge. Brandon Crist's line is modestly anticipatory—it is one designed to serve to set up our closing couplet, and I went for it in the end.

This is where we are:

Our dreams as disparate as our days uniform,	*Michael C. Rush*
We crave a lovely scandal with someone well-known;	*Angela Ball*
Midnight champagne, penthouse lit by thunderstorm,	*Christine Rhein*
In this version of darkness, we are never alone.	*Elizabeth Solsburg*

If marriage is a cage, we can force the lock, but he	*Christine Rhein*
Clutches the key, a jailer too stubborn to learn	*Patricia Smith*
To read the graffiti. If need be, he can turn	*Paul Michelsen*
A bouquet to a wreath. Then we will be	*Poem Today*

Two mourners arguing terms of interment. We must	*Angela Ball*
Appease our lust, our momentary bliss subject to	*Berwyn Moore*
The rules of engagement. The conflicts of lust. Just	*Joe Lawlor*
Look at the way they look at us. As though we're too	*Brandon Crist*

Line thirteen, our penultimate line, must end in "if he can" (or "if she can").

Thank you, everyone, for sticking with this process or for joining us belatedly. It is quite a collaborative exercise to construct a sonnet in fifteen weeks. What we create is bound to be worthy of study. Good luck to all! And happy new year.

Deadline: noon on Sunday, January 3.

A Plot Twist—or Two

January 5, 2016

Here are the finalists, as I saw it, for line thirteen:

Look at the way they look at us. As though we're too
Mad in our pursuit. Love save us if he can!

Millicent Caliban

Look at the way they look at us. As though we're too
Precipitous with a plot, as if he can

Charise Hoge

Look at the way they look at us. As though we're too
Wasteful with wishes. The jailer wonders if he can

Paul Michelsen

Look at the way they look at us. As though we're too
Slow to choose something from the menu. If he can

M. H. Perry

Look at the way they look at us. As though we're too
Free—too free! And, jealous, he'll jail us if he can

Michael C. Rush

All of these lines have their attractions. Charise Hoge's "Precipitous with a plot, as if he can" gets the nod because in its alliterative way it continues the suspension that we initiated in the previous line. The word "plot" in particular is good to have, denoting as it does either a conspiracy or a narrative line. Second-place honors go to M. H. Perry's "Slow to choose something from the menu. If he can," which has the charm of whimsy but is undeniably real—a vivid simile.

Line fourteen promises to be not only our ultimate line but a line on which much emphasis will fall. The only requirement: the line must end with the word "Man" (or "man" or "the wrongs of Man").

And now for the second plot twist of the day. Let's do something different this week. I want to propose a fourteenth line, and this is my candidate:

Trust ourselves to write the wrongs of Man.

In advocating it I would point to the pun on "write" ("right") and the strong meter—an opening spondee ("trust" rhyming with "just," "lust," and "must" above) followed by four robust iambs. And it seems to bring all to a conclusion that, I hope, does justice to the complexities of previous lines.

Now (if we accept my candidate for line fourteen), what does our effort "mean"? What does it add up to? Please feel free, this week and next, to venture your opinion and even offer a succinct analysis—as though the poem were by a deceased person of great interest. We also need a title, so keep that in mind. And by the way, I can also promise a revelation next week.

Here's our poem (tentatively):

Our dreams as disparate as our days uniform,	*Michael C. Rush*
We crave a lovely scandal with someone well-known;	*Angela Ball*
Midnight champagne, penthouse lit by thunderstorm,	*Christine Rhein*
In this version of darkness, we are never alone.	*Elizabeth Solsburg*
If marriage is a cage, we can force the lock, but he	*Christine Rhein*
Clutches the key, a jailer too stubborn to learn	*Patricia Smith*
To read the graffiti. If need be, he can turn	*Paul Michelsen*
A bouquet to a wreath. Then we will be	*Poem Today*
Two mourners arguing terms of interment. We must	*Angela Ball*
Appease our lust, our momentary bliss subject to	*Berwyn Moore*
The rules of engagement. The conflicts of lust. Just	*Joe Lawlor*
Look at the way they look at us. As though we're too	*Brandon Crist*
Precipitous with a plot, as if we can	*Charise Hoge*
Trust ourselves to write the wrongs of man.	*David Lehman*

Congratulations to all the winners and thanks to all good-hearted participatnts whether you've been with us from line one or have joined us since.

Deadline: noon, Sunday, January 9.

The Unmasking

January 12, 2016

For the title of our sonnet, I chose "Jailbreak," Millicent Caliban's suggestion, because in one word it summarizes the most compelling action in our poem. Second place: Berwyn Moore's "The Novelist," for reasons given below. Third place: Michael C. Rush's "The Key," because it is the crucial noun in our second stanza.

Best commentary: A tie between Angela Ball's "black box" argument and Millicent Caliban's brilliant line-by-line analysis. From Angela: "We are confined by a dark universe that keeps us in solitary. A black box, if you will, from which we attempt to write (and paint, dance, play) ourselves free." According to Millicent, "Stanza two implies that marriage can be the antithesis of erotic romance when it becomes a 'cage' or prison. The 'jailer' is the restrictive convention of monogamy. If we remain in a loveless marriage, we are buried alive; that is, 'terms of interment' (rather than 'endearment')."

Here is the revelation I promised, an unmasking. All along our sonnet has conformed to the line endings of a sonnet by W. H. Auden. The sonnet is entitled "The Novelist." (Look it up in your *Collected Auden*.) Berwyn Moore deserves hearty congratulations for suggesting the same title, whether she arrived at it by uncanny intuition, on the basis of our poem, or because she knows her Auden. Mega kudos.

Note: There is an anomaly. I erred when it came to assigning the end words for lines seven and eight; I flipped the proper order. Therefore, the second stanza of our sonnet does not conform strictly to the pattern of Auden's poem.

This, then, is what we wrote:

Jailbreak

Our dreams as disparate as our days uniform,   *Michael C. Rush*
We crave a lovely scandal with someone well-known;   *Angela Ball*

Midnight champagne, penthouse lit by thunderstorm, *Christine Rhein*
In this version of darkness, we are never alone. *Elizabeth Solsburg*

If marriage is a cage, we can force the lock, but he *Christine Rhein*
Clutches the key, a jailer too stubborn to learn *Patricia Smith*
To read the graffiti. If need be, he can turn *Paul Michelsen*
A bouquet to a wreath. Then we will be *Poem Today*

Two mourners arguing terms of interment. We must *Angela Ball*
Appease our lust, our momentary bliss subject to *Berwyn Moore*
The rules of engagement. The conflicts of lust. Just *Joe Lawlor*

Look at the way they look at us. As though we're too *Brandon Crist*
Precipitous with a plot, as if we can *Charise Hoge*
Dig up the words to write the wrongs of man. *Lehman, Solsburg, Michelsen*

I'm amending line fourteen to reflect suggestions from Elizabeth Solsburg and Paul Michelsen. (The line originally was "Trust ourselves to write the wrongs of man." I want also to acknowledge Charise Hoge for pointing out that a third sense of "plot"—as in a burial plot—enhances line thirteen. This argues in favor of the idiomatic "dig up" in line fourteen.

Some thoughts about the poem . . . and a peek at next week:

The last four words of our poem echo Auden's, so in more ways than one we're acknowledging a literary debt and inviting readers to read the two poems side by side—or as scholars say, intertextually. And here's the paradox: An important element of our experiment is that, by proceeding line by line, we wrote our poem entirely without conscious reference to Auden's poem. Nevertheless, the two poems are connected—formally and perhaps in other ways as well.

This is the sort of exercise that Auden himself enjoyed. He believed that word games can be a more reliable source of inspiration than conscious intention. A second theory our experiment tests is whether anomaly, paradox, error, and accident (all of which have come into play) can prove beneficial to a poem.

Like others I feel that one subject of our poem is fiction: the dreams in line one, the fantasy of a scandal, the double hypotheticals in stanzas two and four, the imperative in stanza three. The whole poem is taking place in a universe of extreme contingency: our characters live in metaphor. We unmask ourselves, in the poem's closing couplet, as writers struggling to create amid uncertainty and doubt.

Patricia Smith surmises that an unnamed "she" floats around here somewhere, and Millicent Caliban argues that the "our" and "we" in stanza one may be "the speaker referring to herself in the plural." I find myself nodding my head in agreement. I can also imagine that the jailer in stanza two may refer not only to "the restrictive convention of monogamy" but also to the husband in a loveless or oppressive marriage.

In using unidentified pronouns, we're doing something John Ashbery likes to do in the belief that all pronouns are or can be aspects of the single self, as all the characters in a dream are versions of oneself. The two unadorned declarative statements made in the poem may hold the key: "We crave a lovely scandal" and "We must / Appease our lust." But here the "we" has broadened out to speak for all poets who resort to fantasy to escape from sad actuality.

For next week: (1) Since we seem to be in the realm of the hypothetical as well as the virtual, I say: if we liked the poem enough to publish it, we would need a pseudonym. Suggestions, anyone? Ownership is joint. (2) I will come up with a new project for us, but I'd love to hear from people about forms or exercises you would favor.

Great thanks to all for a most stimulating discussion.

Erase and Change

January 19, 2016

For our next poem, Berwyn Moore would like us to compose a cento, and Paul Michelsen advances the idea of erasure as a method of composition. Combining these suggestions, I propose that we follow this procedure, line by line:

Nominate a line lifted from a poem by a deceased poet who wrote in English. Erase at least one word in the line and/or substitute a word or two. Bonus credit for including an anagram of one word in the previous line. Wit, surprise, profundity, ingenuity, and beauty will be valued. Length will be determined as the lines dictate.

Let me get us started by suggesting a first line. Any of these three, below, will work. Please indicate which your second line is based on:

The road of excess leads to the bliss of solitude

—Based on "The road of excess leads to the palace of wisdom" (Blake) and "the bliss of solitude" (Wordsworth)

Guns fret not at their chamber's narrow doom

—Based on "Nuns fret not at their convent's narrow room" (Wordsworth)

Thus the con artist makes cowboys of us all

—Based on "Thus conscience does make cowards of us all" (Shakespeare)
    Deadline: midnight, Sunday, January 24.

The Mood of Doom, Where Guns Are Snug

January 26, 2016

Angela Ball takes the honors this week. Choosing the Wordsworth-based opening line (which I mistakenly attributed last week to John Keats), Angela suggests this second line:

Guns fret not at their chamber's narrow doom
Snug in our amber mood, we take too little care of what they do.

Angela explains that line two is adapted from the end of one line and the beginning of another in Shakespeare. Note that the first word in her line ("Snug") is an anagram of the first word in line one ("Guns"). Not to mention that "doom" returns as "mood."

Second place: Berwyn Moore, for her line based on Keats's wonderful poem beginning "This living hand, now warm and capable":

Guns fret not at their chamber's narrow doom,
warm and capable in the icy license of the tomb.

The line conjoins part of Keats's first line with the phrase "and in the icy silence of the tomb." It adds to the pleasure that "license" is an anagram of "silence," the word Keats uses.

Bronze medal: Patricia Smith for a line adapted from Walt Whitman's "Song of Myself":

Guns fret not at their chamber's narrow doom
They delight in the rush of the streets

Whitman's line is "The delight alone or in the rush of the streets, or along the fields and hillsides."

Honorable mention to Millicent Caliban:

The road of excess leads to the bliss of solitude:
Alone, alone, all all alone with wine upon my couch.

The first half of the line is taken from Coleridge's "The Rime of the Ancient Mariner," while the prepositional phrase concluding the line alludes to the couch in the first line of the final stanza of Wordsworth's "I Wandered Lonely as Cloud," from which "the bliss of solitude" comes.

I am grateful for the votes that one of my own entries received:

The road of excess leads to the bliss of solitude
And breeds the fine delight that fathers thought

Much of the line is lifted from Gerard Manley Hopkins: "The fine delight that fathers thought; the strong."

For next week, we need an apt third line. The task is to lift a line from an admired poem of the past, then to change that line in an interesting way, with extra points if your line includes an anagram of a word in the previous line. Even better if line three were to rhyme with either "doom" or "do." We are traveling in the unknown with this exercise. Let's have fun and recognize our destination when they get there if not before.

Deadline: noon, January 31.

A Break with Tradition

February 2, 2016

This week we break with tradition and award the laurels to Elizabeth Solsburg for a two-line entry:

Here is the street where frightened children prowl
About their buried innocence, and race

The lines play on two lines from a poem by Stephen Vincent Benét (1898–1943), a poet and writer with an impressive reputation in his own lifetime who went out of fashion and is too little read today. "Race" scrambles "care" in the previous line. Benét's lines:

Here is the strait where eyeless fishes swim
About their buried idol, drowned so cold

Benét is the author of "The Devil and Daniel Webster," a story (and play) that used to be universally read. Benét, who wrote the poem that concludes with the line "Bury my heart at Wounded Knee," served as judge of the Yale Series of Younger Poets for a decade and helped that series achieve its preeminence among first-book competitions.

I like the way Ms. Solsburg retains the structure of Benét's lines while making strategic changes in nouns ("street" for "strait" and "innocence" for "idol"), an adjective ("frightened" for "eyeless"), and a verb ("prowled" for "swim"). It is a good method with the added virtue that it acknowledges its ancestry rather than trying to conceal it. It may be that the paradox of our endeavor here is that we are consciously breaking with the tradition that feeds our effort.

Be that as it may, it is good to call attention to Benét—and to another such unsung poet, Robinson Jeffers (1887–1962), the source of a couple of Patricia Smith's entries. This one wins second place:

Will mood or gun shorten the years, waiting for death anew?

Here is Jeffers's line: "Will shorten the week of waiting for death, there is game without talons."

(Note to Patricia: I'd modify the line to get rid of the dangling participle and make it even more emphatically an echo of Jeffers's "Hurt Hawks": "Will mood or gun shorten the week of waiting for death?" What say you?)

Third place goes to Berwyn Moore for

We hold them as we may, a force in the mind's womb.

"A force," she points out, is an anagram of "care of." This witty scramble is worthy of the poet whose line it is based on. "To hold you as I may, in my mind's womb" is from "Where I've Been All My Life" by the late Carolyn Kizer (1925–2014). Carolyn, a wonderful poet, was also an effective advocate of the art. In 1966, she was appointed director of literary programs for the then-brand-new National Endowment for the Arts.

This, then, is where we are now:

Guns fret not at their chamber's narrow doom.   *DL*
Snug in our amber mood, we take too little care of what they do.   *Angela Ball*
Here is the street where frightened children prowl   *Elizabeth Solsburg*
About their buried innocence, and race   *Elizabeth Solsburg*

For next week . . . we need a line that completes the clause that begins "and race." The line must lift, and play with, a line lifted from a poem by an earlier poet. The line may—for the internal logic of our poem—include an anagram of a word from the previous line. It may also rhyme with any of four words: "doom," "do" (or "they do"), "prowl," and "race." That seems like a lot to accomplish except when you consider that the ingenuity needed to fulfill these conditions may produce, almost without the writer knowing it, an arresting image, thought, line.

Thank you, everyone. I follow the site closely and am grateful not only for the entries but also for the comments.

Deadline: Sunday, February 7, noon, any time zone.

Ruby Tuesday

February 9, 2016

Loving the anagrammatic transformation of "buried" into "rubied," I was torn between Patricia Smith's "Among rubied tenements now fallen into disrepair" and Paul Michelsen's "About the rubied ledge from which our darlings jump too soon." Patricia's line derived from Robert Duncan's poem "The Temple of the Animals"; Paul modified James Tate's line "soon your darling jumps" from "Coming Down Cleveland Avenue."

I do admire rubies in a poem, in their natural state as nouns or in their adjectival form, perhaps because a favorite verse from the King James Version of the Bible is this one, from Proverbs (31:10): "Who can find a virtuous woman? for her price is far above rubies."

Following the lead of certain Iowa caucus precincts, I decided on a coin toss and Paul's line prevailed. Besides, it's nice to have Tate acknowledged on the very week we held a memorial tribute to the late poet at the New School in New York City.

The bronze medal goes to Angela Ball for "To disappear like chess pieces, prisoners all," based on lines from Major Jackson's "On Disappearing": "It's too bad war makes people / disappear like chess pieces, and that prisons / turn prisoners into movie endings."

One aspect of our current enterprise that pleases me much is the attention we are drawing to worthy poets of the past and present. Just this week we have had "reefers" (*Newsweek* shorthand for "references" or "allusions," circa 1983) to Tate, Duncan, and Jackson, but also James Schuyler, William Bronk, Alan Dugan, Robert Frost, H.D., and Edna St. Vincent Millay, among others. I say: bravo. Hats off to these poets and to our team of collaborators, whose ingenuity is matched by their knowledge of pleasurable if little-known poets, such as the underrated Mr. Bronk. Well, they're all underrated, in a sense, even Frost.

Here, then, is where we are. I propose, as you'll see, a stanza break after line two:

Guns fret not at their chamber's narrow doom.   *DL*
Snug in our amber mood, we take too little care of what they do.   *Angela Ball*

Here is the street where frightened children prowl   *Elizabeth Solsburg*
About their buried innocence, and race   *Elizabeth Solsburg*

About the rubied ledge from which our darlings jump too soon.   *Paul Michelsen*

Now, for the sake of symmetry if for no other reason, I am looking for a line that bears a similar relation to its source line as "Guns fret not at their chamber's narrow doom" does to Wordsworth's "Nuns fret not at their convent's narrow room." An anagram is a plus but not absolutely necessary. The winning line will be revealed on February 16, two days after Valentine's Day and a day after the birth of composer Harold Arlen, so think of that!

Deadline: Sunday, February 14, at noon.

Blues in the Night

February 16, 2016

I write this on February 15, the birthday of the composer Harold Arlen, who wrote the music for *The Wizard of Oz* and for such great songs as "Blues in the Night," "Come Rain or Come Shine," and "That Old Black Magic."

We have no fewer than three winning entries this week.

Charise Hoge supplies the first line of the new three-line stanza that emerged. Charise proffers

The sin rests its cheek upon the ground and furrows a cruel stamp.

The line is based on "The wind rests its cheek upon the ground and feels the cool damp" from "Hymn to Life" by James Schuyler, who is indeed as "remarkable" a poet as Cherise says.

Patricia Smith contributes our second line:

When worrisome things lead them to leap in the night,

which is based on Johnny Mercer's lyric for Arlen's "Blues in the Night": A woman is a "worrisome thing / who'll leave you to sing" the deep dark blues in the night.

Smith gets an assist on line three, which is Angela Ball's inventive adaptation of two lines from Arlen songs:

Mama am and am, sings, "Love lived twists deepest blue."

The line derives from "Blues in the Night" (lyric by Johnny Mercer) and, I think, "Between the Devil and the Deep Blue Sea" (lyric by Ted Koehler).

So here's where we are:

Guns fret not at their chamber's narrow doom.   *DL*
Snug in our amber mood, we take too little care of what they do.   *Angela Ball*

Here is the street where frightened children prowl   *Elizabeth Solsburg*
About their buried innocence, and race   *Elizabeth Solsburg*

About the rubied ledge from which our darlings jump too soon.   *Paul Michelsen*
The sin rests its cheek upon the ground and furrows a cruel stamp.   *Charise Hoge*

When worrisome things lead them to leap in the night,   *Patricia Smith*
Mama am and am, sings, "Love lived twists deepest blue."   *Angela Ball*

The strategy last week worked so well that I advocate doing it again. Write a line that refashions an earlier line—the way that, say, "Dope springs eternal in the American West" plays on Alexander Pope's "Hope springs eternal in the human breast." Have fun with it.

And let's see what happens. We're only six lines away from the length of a sonnet, although an unconventional one most certainly.

Deadline: Sunday, February 21, noon (any time zone).

Papa Joins Mama

February 23, 2016

Perhaps it was inevitable that what started out as a friendly competition turned in the end to a celebration of literary collaboration. No fewer than six submitted lines moved me, and when I put them together, I felt that we had a finished poem that worked nicely in two-line stanzas.

The first three lines are from Berwyn Moore:

Papa tumbles down borrowed steps, then sleeps
And Papa sheds his birthright of collards and rat tails.
And Papa swallows moonshine with a hush-hush hoot.

All three are based on Gwendolyn Brooks's poem "The Sundays of Satin-Legs Smith" as we continue our practice of paying homage to the poets we admire.

There then follows this line, derived from Emily Dickinson, by Charise Hoge:

Then wrings, then croons, fraught by birds

Two last-day submissions struck me as forming a wonderful conclusive stanza: Patricia Smith's "Now the darlings we smiled at are most of them dead" (from Siegfried Sassoon) followed Elizabeth Solsburg's "O plaintive singer of the day's last light," based on a line in Keats's "To Sleep."

Now all that's left for us to do is to come up with a title. Please submit one by noon on Sunday, February 28. The best title will be announced next Tuesday along with the ground rules for a new round of "Next Line, Please," with a new prompt.

Here's our poem, which has eight authors. I bet I can get it published. Of course, it *is* published, right here and now, but I suspect I can interest

a magazine in printing or broadcasting it. First, though, we need a title.
One that occurs to me is "Sonnet." But perhaps we can do better.

Guns fret not at their chamber's narrow doom.   *DL*
Snug in our amber mood, we take too little care of what they do.   *Angela Ball*

Here is the street where frightened children prowl   *Elizabeth Solsburg*
About their buried innocence, and race   *Elizabeth Solsburg*

About the rubied ledge from which our darlings jump too soon.   *Paul Michelsen*
The sin rests its cheek upon the ground and furrows a cruel stamp.   *Charise Hoge*

When worrisome things lead them to leap in the night,   *Patricia Smith*
Mama am and am, sings, "Love lived twists deepest blue."   *Angela Ball*

Papa tumbles down borrowed steps, then sleeps,   *Berwyn Moore*
And Papa sheds his birthright of collards and rat tails,   *Berwyn Moore*

And Papa swallows moonshine with a hush-hush hoot   *Berwyn Moore*
Then wrings, then croons, fraught by birds.   *Charise Hoge*

Now the darlings we smiled at are most of them dead,   *Patricia Smith*
O plaintive singer of the day's last light!   *Elizabeth Solsburg*

Heaven, Hope, or a Ghostly Sight

March 1, 2016

A lot of the submitted titles for our sonnet seemed very appealing to me, and I am really taken with Millicent Caliban's congratulatory note to us as well as her nomination of Blake's phrase. Of the various titles suggested, I went in the end with "Blues in the Night," which was proposed by Carey James. It was, as noted, the title of one weekly post, and arguably the central moment in our poem. I guess I am also partial to the habit of titling poems after popular songs.

For next week, I propose that participants choose one of these lines and make it the first line of a new and succinct poem. Each of the lines is the first line of an Emily Dickinson poem:

Heaven is what I cannot reach!
Hope is a subtle glutton
The only ghost I ever saw

Do yourself a favor and do NOT read the Dickinson poem in question until after you've completed your poem. It's hard to compete with her. DO read other Dickinson poems and notice the many ways she can develop an initial premise—and always with admirable brevity.

This is a one-week contest.

I also ask each participant to email at least one friend with the invitation to join in. It is wonderful to have a small but dedicated cadre, but wouldn't it be great if we could introduce new blood and brains?

Deadline: Sunday, March 6, at noon. Good luck everyone—and thank you for taking part.

Galloping Ghosts

March 8, 2016

The prompt for this week was to take a first line by Emily Dickinson and make it the first line of a new poem in her manner.

Of the three Dickinson lines proffered, the three best entries all began with Dickinson's "The only ghost I ever saw." I decided to split the top prize three ways.

Angela Ball, who alters Dickinson's line somewhat, gives us in her opening lines an antithesis that is perfectly in line with Dickinson's practice. And the concluding lines, within quote marks, constitute a most apposite riddle: who is speaking?

I only saw a ghost but once—
Or—rather—he saw me—
From high window with basket
And pulley—I lowered gingernuts

To skirls of little caps and bonnets—
Fleeting plumage paused to feed.
And then—the insubstantial voice—"One day—
should you descry the means—
please lower some to me."

Millicent Caliban gives us these beautiful quatrains. The metrical regularity, the rightness of tone, the pivot on the word "Yet," and the excellent concluding rhyme are virtues:

The only ghost I ever saw
Paid no regard to me,
Vouchsafed no revelation
Nor bespoke eternity.

Yet instantly I knew him,
Could feel his icy clutch
As if to paralyze my heart
Without the need to touch.

Sarah Paley writes:

The only ghost I ever saw
studied me head to toe
She patted my dark circles—paused—
poked gently at my nose

Are you really here? She pondered
Of course I am. I'm me!
twenty years now I've wondered
what was she trying to see?

I admire the rhyme of "ghost" and "paused" and love the way "I'm me" revises Dickinson's "I'm Nobody."

Honorable mention goes to Noreen Ellis for her concise and haunting lines:

Hope is a subtle glutton
Faith, a satiated tart
Love, hungry, devours both.

There were so many solid submissions that I am convinced that Emily Dickinson's fragments will supply the ground for future contests.

Next week there will be a new competition. Stay tuned!

Spring Forward

March 15, 2016

By this time next week we will have officially crossed the threshold into spring, in whose honor may I propose that we engage in a game of competitive haikus.

The idea is to write a technically correct stanza: three lines with five syllables in line one, seven syllables in line two, and five syllables in line three. The poem needs to have the word spring in it. Otherwise, the poem should have concrete details only.

Enter as often as you wish. The setting may be urban or bucolic, on any continent, at any time of day or night, any day of the week.

You may rhyme.

Deadline: Sunday, March 20, at noon.

Have fun with it!

This Week's Haiku to Become Next Week's Tanka

March 22, 2016

We garnered 103 comments comprising more than that number of haiku entries (some comments contained more than one haiku). And many submissions were inventive, clever, and informed by a most convincing clamor for spring, the real thing, to turn up!

I chose this quartet of haikus from Eduardo Ramos Ruiz:

Aubade of springtime:
A young western scrub jay cries—
Where has winter gone?

The color of spring
In summer vegetables—
Winter is pickled

A tropic spring night,
Making Mole poblano—
We drank wine with ice

Beetroots at harvest:
Spring of picker's purple hands—
Taproot stains for life

But I wanted to single out other worthy entries such as Sarahsarai's whimsical

On Lexington Ave.
Spring is just another word
for "You wanted Park."

And Pat Blake's anthropomorphic extravaganza:

I melted on him.
Nothing accumulated.
Spring undid winter.

And John Weerden's celebration of red:

Girl in a red dress
picking poppies in springtime,
O pick me, pick me

And Charles Bingham's local habitation and a name:

Whales feed on herring,
flowers bloom; spring is here in
Sitka, Alaska.

And Tyler Goldman's masterly seven-syllable middle line:

After the false spring:
the spring. The ducks (here too soon)
have already left

And Winona Winkler Wendth's "Green":

Bent grass knows only
bending—not who lay with whom
or why just that spring

And Karen Topham's begonias:

Begonias scarlet
Prove too much spring to ignore
Buy three, maybe four

And Leonard Kress's mini-ode to jazz:

Walk to the river
Play "Round Midnight" in your mind
Miles to go till spring

And Marissa Despain's excursion into gastronomy:

Sibling Rivalry

Japanese eggplant:
slimmer sweeter sibling of
Italian eggplant.

I tried my own hand at the exercise in lines that turned out to be less optimistic than most. My title: "The Odds":

Spring is in the dice
If what is past is prologue—
But is it? (Cat's eyes.)

Kudos to everyone.

Now let's build on this foundation. For next week, I ask you to pick one of Eduardo Ramos Ruiz's four haiku—and to add a two-line stanza, each line consisting of exactly seven syllables. The result will be a tanka. The tanka is a Japanese form with a rich heritage; Basho was a master, and the Columbia professor Donald Keene is a great advocate and explainer of what can be done with the form, which was a favorite way for Japanese poets—such as Basho and contemporaries—to collaborate.

For example, one poet would write a three-line-stanza, the next poet would write a two-line stanza, and the third poet would write a new three-line stanza without seeing anything but the two-line stanza. In such manner the poem would be extended and would take twists and turns inevitably as each poet operated with limited knowledge of the renga in progress—renga being the Japanese term for such a collaborative poem.

In your submissions, please indicate which of Eduardo Ramos Ruiz's haiku you've chosen and then enter your two seven-syllable lines.

Deadline: Noon on Sunday, March 27.

Let the Renga Reign

March 29, 2016

For this week, poets were asked to compose two seven-syllable lines that would build on the haiku by Eduardo Ramos Ruiz that took first place last week. The addition of two such lines fulfills the requirements of the Japanese verse form known as the tanka. Eduardo's winning entry consisted of four separate haiku, and contributors were told to pick any of the four for their tanka.

Each of the three two-line stanzas that I liked the most chose the same haiku as its base. Here they are:

Karen Topham:

A tropic spring night,
Making Mole poblano—
We drank wine with ice

Zinfandel: dark, fruity, rich,
Pairs well, or so he told me

Dick Humbird:

A tropic spring night,
Making Mole poblano—
We drank wine with ice

Then smirked, because it was red
Loving the desecration

Angela Ball:

A tropic spring night,
Making Mole poblano—
We drank wine with ice

Below clouds' close voyages—
moon tipped on its slender back

    Meanwhile, Eduardo Ramos Ruiz provided a new haiku to allow us to extend our tankas into a renga: Japanese linked verse, consisting of alternating haiku and tanka stanzas. Here, then, are three different versions of our renga:

(1)

A tropic spring night,
Making Mole poblano—
We drank wine with ice

Zinfandel: dark, fruity, rich,
Pairs well, or so he told me

The scent of chiles,
Chocolate and canela—
Vivaldi: salud!

(2)

A tropic spring night,
Making Mole poblano—
We drank wine with ice

Then smirked, because it was red
Loving the desecration

The scent of chiles,
Chocolate and canela—
Vivaldi: salud!

(3)

A tropic spring night,
Making Mole poblano—
We drank wine with ice

Below clouds' close voyages—
moon tipped on its slender back

The scent of chiles,
Chocolate and canela—
Vivaldi: salud!

You, dear reader, are asked to vote for your favorite . . . and to extend the renga further by proposing two more seven-syllable lines. Ideally your two lines should relate to the haiku just before it—while deviating in some significant way (landscape, weather, time of day) from the first haiku in the sequence.

Deadline: Sunday, April 3, noon.

"April Is the Cruelest Month, [Because]"

April 5, 2016

We have an exciting new project on our hands. But first, here are two versions of our renga, one provided by Millicent Caliban:

A tropic spring night,
Making Mole poblano—
We drank wine with ice

Zinfandel: dark, fruity, rich,
Pairs well, or so he told me

The scent of chiles,
Chocolate and canela—
Vivaldi: salud!

Senses primed for sweet and tart
Will yield to bliss before dawn.

    . . . and the other by Paul Michelsen:

A tropic spring night,
Making Mole poblano—
We drank wine with ice

Below clouds' close voyages—
moon tipped on its slender back

The scent of chiles,
Chocolate and canela—
Vivaldi: salud!

Wash out the taste of winter
With this: La Primavera

While the renga as a form can theoretically be extended indefinitely, this seems a good place to suspend the effort.

Our next contest has to do with the current month. I want us to take a look at the famous opening of T. S. Eliot's "The Waste Land":

April is the cruelest month, breeding

Now remove the word "breeding," substitute an invisible "because," and write a worthy second line.

Deadline: Sunday, April 10, at 5 p.m.

T. S. Eliot: Still Undefeated

April 12, 2016

The prompt for this week was T. S. Eliot's famous first line—"April is the cruelest month, breeding"—minus the word "breeding." Participants were asked to imagine an invisible "because" and to provide a second line, an alternative to Eliot's "Lilacs out of the dead land, mixing."

It must be said that T. S. Eliot remains the true victor in the competition. In fact his opening sentence, stretched out over four lines—"April is the cruelest month, breeding / Lilacs out of the dead land, mixing / Memory and desire, stirring / Dull roots with spring rain"—exemplifies free verse at its craftiest. Just look at the work those participles ("breeding," "mixing," and "stirring") do to propel the reader onward while at the same time forcing a trembling pause at the end of each line. The pause at the end of line one, for example, isolates a word of tremendous importance in Eliot's vision of modern life—a vision in which, except for saints and saintly fools, most of us are breeders, and love is not a requisite for copulation.

Speaking of participles and the work they do, I liked Beth Gylys's

April is the cruelest month,
pollen-gagged, marching into May

best of the entries because of the double meaning of "marching"—and the suggestion that time is of the speedy essence, marching past April as past an unimportant parenthesis on the way to May and true spring.

Aya Dela Peña's entry

April is the cruelest month, because
A scribe's worthier temptress than a promise of applause.

may not work as verse, but as prose it is as fascinating as it is grammatically implausible. The metaphors—scribe, temptress, applause—suggest a power-packed allegory of sensuality and performance. I hope the writer elaborates the line into a short poem.

Angela Ball's

April is the cruelest month because
Of the new: rills, pails of lilacs, pairs.

offers what seems to me the strongest second line from the point of view of sheer metrical dexterity—the way the accents are distributed among the syllables, the preponderance of which consists of monosyllables. The only word with more than one syllable is "lilacs"—a clever and subtle allusion to the second line of "The Waste Land."

Honorable mention goes to Eduardo Ramos Ruiz:

April is the cruelest month,
Its march unveils rot and rust

For next week, why don't we undertake to write a one-line poem—or a one-sentence prose poem—under the title "Lace Curtain" (or "Behind the Lace Curtain")? I am thinking of the name of a once-popular drink that consisted half of vodka and half of gin. That is one direction to which the title points, but there can be many others, no?

Deadline: Sunday, April 17, at 5 p.m.

Behind the Curtain

April 19, 2016

The prompt: What can you do succinctly with a ready-made title, "Lace Curtain"? I liked best two efforts at defining the phrase: Pat Blake's in the language of the dictionary:

Lace Cur-tain (noun)

The boundary dividing what we think of ourselves and what others think; a
  veil, a mist, a tattered dream.

and Millicent Caliban's in an allegorical figure:

Lace Curtain

Behind a respectable window, she's always there invisible, recording our
  indiscretions

　　Runner-up Katie Belanger impressed me with her alliterative and rhythmic line:

Lace Curtain

One sip to sink, rub raw the surface, scrape off the shield.

　　And Aya Dela Peña took off on a narrative impulse:

Me too, she laughed, overeasy, smacking her lips wet with bitter wine and
  caustic words before drowning into the cackling night with a measly tip:
  a tapered hip.

So many other worthy entries leave me convinced that the exercise is a good one and worth doing again, perhaps with another phrase lifted from my book of cocktail recipes.

For next week, I invite all poets to take your name, any part of your name, and use it as the point of departure for a brief poem. For example, in my own case, I could write of King David in the books of Samuel in the Old Testament, of the medieval "leman," of Governor Herbert Lehman in office during the New Deal, or of the collapse of Lehman Brothers in 2008—or I could build a poem out of anagrams (avid diva; he-man?) or an acrostic.

Deadline: Sunday, April 24, 5 p.m.

The Pen Name Is Mightier Than the Word

April 26, 2016

This week the prompt was to use your name as the point of departure for a poem. First prize goes to Millicent Caliban for her cri de coeur:

Nom de plume

A feather name is light.
It flies without the burden of an acknowledged self.
To choose your name is to set free
What else would be concealed within.
Thus can I speak with borrowed voices,
Which will not be confounded with that other
Who lives and breathes the common air;
That one who, once arrived, must claim her baggage.
I am duty-free, without accustomed tags or labels,
Can summon diverse spirits to soar, or maybe sink,
But never will be trapped in any sordid tree.

Millicent Caliban is so evidently a pen name, combining the heroine of a Restoration comedy with the male brute in "The Tempest," that the subject of the pen-name, or nom de plume, turned out to be ideally set up for her. The poem seems filled with clues and with imagery that suits: to differentiate the free but secret self from the "baggage" of a worldly identity is to be "duty-free, without accustomed tags or labels" (with an extra nice pun on "customs"). I am a little mystified by the sordid tree that completes the poem, though I admire the way it picks up the rhyme of "free" in the third line.

Second place goes to Paul Michelsen for his cento—the last letters of which spell out his last name:

Last, at the end

The birds sing. The bees hum.
I cannot say more than that, can I?
Fade away like a lovely music
Of anybody's sudden death
The world goes by my cage and never sees me
cared for anyone not at all
And the taste of you burnt my mouth with its sweetness.
"Perhaps you can write to me."
Proof of whisperings I refuse to abandon.

    Three-way tie for third, the distinction to be split among Angela Ball's meditation on her given name:

Angela

I often think I've
never quite "gelled"—innocence
wings and returns, quizzical,
cocked at some obtuse
angle. In German, I'm
hard-edged with a hint
of opera. Spanish to
English, the heart calls
out "hello" or "why
did you do that?"

and Eduardo Ramos Ruiz's bilingual anagram poem:

Ode de Muse

Arise dorado aura
amid medusoid dreams,
redo doomed odors.
Arouse razored ideas—

Eros' amorous serum.
Dear Dread, adios!

and Charise Hoge for her "name claim check":

not the paint of cerise
not the squint of an e
not a calamity of s's
not a cha cha that arises
—cease filibuster—phoneticize,
begin in shh . . . end in ease
prescient ahh placed between
r is the trill for knees on bees

For next week . . . I have long treasured tabloid newspapers for their clever headlines, knowing puns, and funny turns of phrase. In today's *New York Post*, for example, the columnist Phil Mushnick wants to score off Major League Baseball's use of replay tape to settle disputed calls—and gets his way, rhetorically at least, when he says that "MLB has reinvented the flat tire."

I ask you to take a phrase from a newspaper, whether a headline or a sentence in an article, and use it to spring a succinct and witty poem. The phrase can be (but doesn't have to be) your poem's epigraph. Or, for example, it can serve as a quotation within your poem.

Deadline: Sunday May 1, 5 p.m.

Walt Whitman's Manly Diet

May 3, 2016

The prompt this week was to write a poem triggered by a newspaper headline or phrase in an article. The entries were good and very ambitious. The winner: Angela Ball for what she does with a phrase that leaped out at her from the day's reading of the *New York Times*. Here is the winning entry:

"Walt Whitman Promoted a Paleo Diet"
—*The New York Times*

Walt, I know which way
your beard is pointing
tonight—toward meat!
Dripping joints of every
description, legs, sides,
stomachs—a manly diet.
But, Walt, every atom
of you as good belongs
to me! Atoms of
blueberries, blackberries,
kumquats, arugula, apples,
the seeds of sunflowers,
bread, effulgent at dawn and
rumbling (if you hold it to an ear)
of ovens. No wonder
you speak of "the sound
of the belch'd words
of my voice." That is indigestion!
Walt, I know I am just a "tripper
and asker," a "puller and hauler,"

but is it really too late
to change your mind? I call
to the thousand responses
of your heart. Death, strong
and delicious word,
is not so appealing in the form
of bloody flesh on a plate!
This gentle call is for you, my love,
for you. It comes from the twenty-ninth
bather. Surely you must know
who is here.

This is a fine poem by any standard, and I am delighted that a "Next Line, Please" prompt quickened it into existence. The poem is quite learned though it wears that learning lightly. Quotations from "Song of Myself" and "Out of the Cradle Endlessly Rocking" are woven into the lines, which sound Whitmanic in the best possible sense of that neologism. The exclamation points, the list of foods, the direct address to the great granddaddy of American poetry, the declaration of love—all contribute to the effect, which puts the poem in the select company of wondrous works that talk to Whitman. (Offhand, for example, I think of poems by Lorca, Pessoa, Hart Crane, Allen Ginsberg, and Lyn Emanuel.)

Thank you to all who wrote or commented. "Next Line, Please" is, it seems to me, not only a pastime but an experiment in the creative mind and an investigation into the roots of poetic inspiration.

For next week, let's write poems about paintings. Go to the local museum, ponder a painting, and write a brief poem about it. Use as your model, if you like, Auden's "Musée des Beaux Arts" in which he writes about Brueghel's *Landscape with the Fall of Icarus*. If you do not have ready access to a good art museum or gallery, exploit the worldwide web's cache of reproductions of wondrous pictures by Raphael, Titian, Tintoretto, Rembrandt, Velázquez, Vermeer, Goya, Manet, Monet, Cézanne, Picasso, and Matisse (to limit myself to a dozen); choose one and make it the subject of your consideration. Please indicate the painter and title of painting with your entry or entries.

Deadline: Sunday, May 8, 5 p.m.

A Familiar Public Place

May 10, 2016

We wrote poems about paintings last week. Inspired by W. H. Auden's "Musée des Beaux Arts," a poem about great paintings, including one by Brueghel, Millicent Caliban takes top prize for this salute to Edward Hopper:

To Edward Hopper, a New Master
(*Automat*, 1927)
with more than a nod to W. H. Auden

How well he understood the need to be alone.
About our failed connections he was never wrong.
He knew one must have world enough and time:
Bright inner space to set against the dark outside,
A familiar public place to sit and think,
While sipping coffee good and strong
That issues from a plated dolphin's mouth.
To stare into a cup that warms an ungloved hand,
To search within for reasons or for grace,
Or seek, when love and hope are gone, what may remain.
The private meditation, how it takes place while others may be sitting
At their separate marble tables, nursing coffee and their secret griefs
    unknown.
No fear they will intrude; they keep the city's custom: each to his own.
One might observe the fetching yellow hat that looks so well at just that angle,
Might suppose she could be gay and sparkling if in a lively crowd,
Seductive like a luscious piece of fruit that lies there tempting in a crystal bowl,
As if she would let others even glimpse what lies beneath her coat of green,
As if she even knew herself all that is there as yet unseen,
Beyond the piercing emptiness and pain.

How sad we can no longer find our solace in an Automat like that.

Second place goes to Charise Hoge for this poem in the triolet form. Note the artful repetition of lines:

Soft Palette

The momentum of water lilies
is round, a resplendent haze
of emergent lucidities.
The momentum of water lilies,
repeating morning reveilles,
underscores Monet's matinees.
The momentum of water lilies
is round, a resplendent haze.

For next week, may I suggest that players write the shortest possible poem of pith and wit under the title "The Judgment of Paris" with this elaborate epigraph, which I take from Edith Hamilton's *Mythology*:

"Hera promised to make him Lord of Europe and Asia; Athena, that he would lead the Trojans to victory against the Greeks and lay Greece in ruins; Aphrodite, that the fairest woman in all the world should be his. Paris, a weakling and something of a coward . . . chose the last. He gave Aphrodite the golden apple."

Deadline: May 15, 6 p.m. Feel free to recruit friends to enter their poems. The competition among the three goddesses strikes me as an unusually compelling subject.

The Judgment of Paris

May 17, 2016

The prompt this week was to write a poem entitled "The Judgment of Paris," with this epigraph from Edith Hamilton: "Hera promised to make him Lord of Europe and Asia; Athena, that he would lead the Trojans to victory against the Greeks and lay Greece in ruins; Aphrodite, that the fairest woman in all the world should be his. Paris, a weakling and something of a coward . . . chose the last. He gave Aphrodite the golden apple."

Angela Ball takes her cue from "the fairest woman in all the world," the "face that launched a thousand ships" (Christopher Marlowe)—the woman that Paris abducted from her husband, Menelaus, king of Sparta, providing all the justification that the Trojan War needed.

Helen

Paris is no prize.
A woman wants a man
who can defend her
come what may—not
a preening aesthete.
Obedient, I swam
with him through
night clubs and salons—
arm candy with a priceless
pedigree. While battles
blaze—and I, my face
at least—get blamed. Why
in Olympus's name
do Gods ensnare soft
mortals in their games?
Perhaps because
we're easily replaced.

I would like also to praise the indefatigable inventiveness of Paul Michelsen, perhaps especially in his poem "The Judgment of Parrots."

My own effort, written before I saw any of the others, was essentially a paraphrase of Edith Hamilton:

The Judgment of Paris

Hera offers him the presidency.
Athena says he can be a hero.
Aphrodite offers him Helen—
Beauty and the consummation
Of desire.

Freud offers an explanation.
Aphrodite is death.
Athena is victory.
Hera is power.
Paris chooses death without knowing it.

He was right to choose the lead casket
As Lear should have chosen Cordelia
As you should choose the third sister in any series.
But Paris, being a coward,
Chooses Helen, and dies.

For next week, why don't we have a contest for the best prompt? Criteria will include appeal, practical effectiveness, originality, "high-concept" clarity and succinctness. I am inviting you all to tell me how to do my job, at least for one week, and I hope you will also feel free to comment on the nominees. Poetry is sometimes thought to be an aristocratic art. Do democracy and poetry go together?

Deadline: Sunday, May 22, 6 p.m.

Prompting a Poem, Dreaming of a Drink

May 24, 2016

The prompt this week: to devise a prompt. Paul Michelsen wins not only for his amazing industry but for his ingenuity. One of Paul's prompts is itself a prose poem, it seems to me. Here it is:

"One of the classic questions interviewers love to ask writers is who they would have to a dinner party if they could invite anyone, living or dead. Write a poem about the dinner party of your dreams. Who would you invite? What would you serve? Who would drink too much? Who would choke on one of your exquisitely prepared hors d'oeuvres? Which one of your guests would you most like to perform the Heimlich maneuver on? Why on Earth would you try doing the Heimlich on someone other than the one who is actually choking? Horrible host, redeem yourself with the kind of brilliant poem only you can write. This is your party after all."

The two runners-up have major virtues.

Berwyn Moore: "Find an unusual or archaic word and make it the springboard for a poem." Berwyn has acted on this prompt herself. The prompt has the virtue of referring us to the Oxford English Dictionary as an unfailing source for poems.

Andrew Paul Wood suggested that the reader "Write a poem titled 'American Democracy' loosely following the structure of Philip Larkin's 'This Be the Verse,' including references to at least three US presidencies from any point in history to the present." This is quite an ambitious assignment. It has the virtue of getting the engaged reader to read Larkin's excellent and still somewhat notorious poem, which begins, "They fuck you up, your mum and dad. / They may not mean to, but they do."

Now, it may be objected that this prompt is guilty of leading the witness—it urges the idea that the "fucked-up" parents and children of Larkin's poem are stand-ins for American democracy, which is implicitly in a sorry state with reference to "at least three" American presidents.

The political is poison for poetry. Nevertheless, in the writing of it, problems can turn into spurs for the imagination.

Under the heading "An invitation to poetry," Mark Doty asks, "What's your dream drink, what goes into making it, and what happens after you have one?" Let's make that our prompt for next week. Think of the poem as a cocktail—or the recipe as a poem. Julie Sheehan has an entire book of poems based on this cocktail conceit.

And now that summer drinks are upon us, the mind turns to such concoctions, and I hereby give notice that I am writing a poem entitled "Cocktail," which is itself a beautiful word if you think about it. My entry begins with "the summer of sangria (a puree of white peaches made the difference), the summer of classic daiquiris (rum, sugar, lime juice in equal measures), the autumn morning bloody marys (hot and spicy but refreshing), the fortified martinis (the ice-cold gin topped by a capful of Laphroaig scotch), the March old fashioned with muddled cherries and a slice of blood orange)."

Let's have your "dream drink" (and feel free to enter more than once) by Sunday, June 5, at 6 p.m.

You Must Get Drunk

June 7, 2016

This week's prompt was to concoct, in verse, a summer drink—tall, cool, refreshing, and partaking perhaps in the spirit of Charles Baudelaire's injunction, "you must get drunk." Here is my translation from the French of his famous prose poem, "Enivrez-vous!" (i.e., "Get Drunk"):

> You must get drunk. That's it: your sole imperative. To protect yourself from the backbreaking, body-bending burdens of time, you must get drunk and stay that way.
>
> But on what? On wine, on poetry, or on virtue, your choice. But get drunk.
>
> And if sometimes, while on the steps of a palace, on the green grass beside a marsh, in the morning solitude of your room, you snap out of it, your drunkenness has worn off, has worn off entirely, then ask the wind, ask an ocean wave, a star, a bird, a clock, every evanescent thing, everything that flies, that groans, that rolls, that sings, that speaks, ask them what time it is; and the wind, the wave, the star, the bird, the clock, will tell you: "It's time to get drunk! To avoid being the martyred slaves of time, get drunk, get drunk and stay that way. On wine, on poetry, or on virtue, your choice."

Millicent Caliban's winning entry gets right into the spirit of things. She presents poetry—the work of Charlie Baudelaire and Johnny Keats, among others—as an intoxicant. Here is her poem, a review of major English and American poets:

Getting Drunk on Poetry

I recommend a dive run by Charlie Baudelaire.
Getting drunk on poetry is the way to cheat despair.
If Johnny Keats is tending bar, tell him, "Easy on the hemlock."

For a divine drink, he knows the source is Hippocrene.
If you'd like your unbrewed liquor in a tankard scooped from pearl
With a twist of debauched dew, Emily Dickinson is your girl.
Roll the words on your tongue to start a drumbeat in your brain.
Take a little Wallace Stevens up straight and try looking at a bird.
Walt Whitman goes down smooth with Dylan Thomas as a chaser,
A glass of Milton on the rocks is paradise gained (or maybe lost).
If a shot of Hopkins makes it too intense, just chill with Frost.
The mundane world begins to fade; you can get high on rhyme.
Charlie has it right, you'd best be tipsy all the time.

The lines about Keats are specific to his "Ode to a Nightingale," and there are smart allusions to works by John Milton and to Robert Frost's last name, but my favorite couplet is the one concerning Emily Dickinson.

Other entries were impressive in ways worth singling out. Paul Michelsen in "Mixed Drinks" collapses glorious dream into humble reality as he slips out of Hitchcock's *North by Northwest* and realizes that his "screwdriver is really only orange juice / This MacGuffin merely a McMuffin." I also love Paul's line from a second poem he posted: "Cliché of the day: Throwing it all away." And by the way, Paul's winning prompt last week included a reference to the Heimlich maneuver—and a few days later I read in the newspaper that Dr. Heimlich, now a nonagenarian, applied his maneuver to save the life of a dinner companion, a very grateful woman in her eighties.

Charise Hoge puns cleverly in her atmospheric "Flashback." Consider: "no ifs, ands . . . cigarette butts / in ashtrays, mixed nuts / marriage on the rocks." And Angela Ball's entry, "What Is That Drink They Are Having Over There?" makes the most of its premise:

My girlfriend and I order cocktails
called, "All of Our Troubles,"
flamingo-pink tinctures
mixed from catastrophe—

I took a break for Memorial Day but am back in the saddle. For next week: Why it's good to be alive—in twenty-five words or less, prose or verse, form or free. Brevity will be valued. Deadline: Sunday, June 13, two days after my birthday, at midnight.

Reasons to Live

June 14, 2016

This week's prompt turned out to be extremely difficult. I asked people to express "why it's good to be alive" in twenty-five words or less, verse or prose.

Here are two excellent responses that could not be more different in tone and verse technique:

Millicent Caliban:

The Afterlife gets mixed reviews,
Eternity can drag.
Our mortal play has wit and pace,
Delight may be achieved through pain,
Serenity through grace.

Berwyn Moore:

Lines for a friend who died from cancer:

And in your last exuberant breath, you knew—
as definite as water or bark—that the reasons
for loving far outweigh the reasons for living.

I admire, too, Angela Ball's "Why It's Good to Be Alive":

Figs from the tree
you planted, bread
from yeast that share
your home, coffee
that serves the rough
word "burlap," excellent
to the tongue.

There were other fine entries from Paul Michelsen, Byron, Charise Hoge, and Patricia Smith. To all, my thanks. I must admit that I made several attempts of my own and was reminded of the list Woody Allen gives in *Manhattan*—a list that includes Cézanne's apples and pears, Groucho Marx, Willie Mays, the second movement of Mozart's *Jupiter Symphony*, Louis Armstrong's "Potato Head Blues," Swedish movies, Flaubert's "Sentimental Education," Marlon Brando, Frank Sinatra, and "the crabs at Sam Wo's."

For reasons of space in this book, we skip to the column of August 23.

Young Lycidas

August 23, 2016

The prompt for this week—to rewrite two to six lines of Milton's "Lycidas"—turned out to be one of the most stimulating we've had in a long time. What wonderful submissions we've received. "Put it in the books," the Mets' radio announcer Howie Rose says after a New York victory. This is one for the books.

I am happy to reveal that from now until the onset of winter, each week's winner will receive a complimentary copy of *The Best American Poetry 2016*, edited by Edward Hirsch.

First place is divided between two different entries. Here is Millicent Caliban's:

So what's the point in striving every week
To pen some verses fit for "Next Line, Please"
While straining every sinew of the mind?
Why not seek pastimes of more common kind,
Abandon art, with YouTube take some ease,
Watch shady porn or kittens tangling skeins?

Which is, as she says, "(De)based on"
Alas! what boots it with uncessant care
To tend the homely, slighted shepherd's trade,
And strictly meditate the thankless Muse?
Were it not better done, as others use,
To sport with Amaryllis in the shade,
Or with the tangles of Neæra's hair?

This happens to be my own favorite quotation from "Lycidas," and the very passage that I undertook to translate into a modern idiom (see below). I admire Millicent's balance of contemporary reference (YouTube, "shady porn") with the noble accents of the master ("While straining every sinew of the mind"). Nicely done.

Cowinner is Berwyn Moore's

So spirals the seeds of the sunflower,
its buttery lattice a mathematical marvel.
Though Helianthos fades at summer's end,
in time our friend will bow his studded head again.

after lines 168–171 of Milton's poem:

So sinks the day-star in the ocean bed,
And yet anon repairs his drooping head,
And tricks his beams, and with new-spangled ore
Flames in the forehead of the morning sky:

Berwyn says her entry was "inspired by the Fibonacci sequence." I like and use the Fibonacci formula, but don't quite see how it applies here. This looks more like an "n + 7" exercise formulated by OuLiPo, the French association of writers and mathematicians devoted to creating new strict literary forms. (I hope Berwyn will elaborate on her method.) In any case, there is something lovely in the alliteration of Berwyn's first line, and the poignancy of "Though Helianthos fades at summer's end" reminds me of my favorite line in Shakespeare's sonnet 18, "And summer's lease hath all too short a date."

First runner-up is Paul Michelsen's eloquent

Another Perfect Day

The sweetest friends make the most bitter ends
Not the first or last perfect day death ruined
Not too young, but too young for our liking
Our preferences no match with those of wild nature.
Once we sang together, now I sing alone,
but tomorrow's silence here will lead to somewhere
else a chorus.

inspired by the following lines:

Bitter constraint and sad occasion dear
Compels me to disturb your season due;
For Lycidas is dead, dead ere his prime,
Young Lycidas, and hath not left his peer.
Who would not sing for Lycidas? he knew
Himself to sing, and build the lofty rhyme.

Here is my own effort to capture the pith and meaning of the lines both Millicent Caliban and I chose:

Why study poetry, major in English, climb the stair-
Way to failure as you struggle with an obsolete art,
And woo a fickle muse, forsaking wealth and fame?
Wouldn't it make better sense to enter the frame
Of the picture, kiss the girl and capture her heart
And glory in every last curl and wave of her hair?

I do not want to leave unmentioned Anna Rowe's strong entry, based on the same lines that inspired Paul Michelsen. Anna's entry referenced the swimmer Ryan Lochte's exploits in the pool and late at night in the 2016 Olympic games in Rio:

Young Lochte, with records left to transcend.
Must we all tweet for Lochte? His testimony
Was drunk, but his races are sober.

This prompted Millicent Caliban's comment: "Who would not tweet for Lycidas?"

Charise Hoge's translation of "For Lycidas, your sorrow, is not dead," into "Wing it after the burn out, some Phoenix-like dawn" deservedly drew ooohs and aahs.

Laura Orem's four-line summary of "Lycidas" starts with an arresting first line: "Dude, you were alive and now you're dead."

I would also praise submissions by "Next Line, Please" regulars Christine Rhein, Patricia Smith, and Elizabeth Solsburg and would like to extend a warm welcome to Kate Saffin and Courtney.

For next week, consider the poem of apology William Carlos Williams wrote under the title, "This Is Just to Say." The poem pivots on the phrase "Forgive me." But after reciting the transgression he has committed—eating the plums that his wife may have been saving for breakfast—the speaker turns penitence into glee as he relishes in the pleasure of the fruit he has eaten. Kenneth Koch wrote a hilarious parody, in which the "I," apologizing for breaking his partner's leg while dancing, admits to having been "clumsy," and then reveals the motive behind his disguised hostility. "I wanted you here in the wards, where I am the doctor!"

Your assignment: write a poem that expresses an insincere, or false, or otherwise remarkable apology. You may use the words "Forgive me" but that is strictly optional. The fruits of transgression have a great history (Genesis, St. Augustine's *Confessions*), but you need not limit yourself to culinary matters.

Deadline: Saturday night, August 27, midnight any time zone.

The Fake Apology

August 30, 2016

This week we wrote fake apologies on the model of William Carlos Williams's "This Is Just to Say," a kind of Post-it-note poem in which the husband apologizes to the wife for eating the plums she had saved for her breakfast.

The responses persuade me that there is fertile ground for the poet in the insincere utterance. Our tendency to lie and distort and revise follows from the inability of the language to discriminate between truth and falsehood: Language is not self-verifying. Fiction is based on just this discrepancy between language and the duplicitous and calculating writer. Discrepancy—or struggle? Writers often describe their writing as a kind of wrestling match with language, as T. S. Eliot does in *Four Quartets*.

My favorite fake apologies are a pair submitted by Marissa Despain:

Congratulations!
I saw your
new book
at a bookstore

and:

Oh no! I forgot
To have your baby. Now
it's too late. Sorry!

Byron helpfully illuminates the appeal of the two: "The subtlety of the first, the concealed hostility of the second." The first depends on the distinction between seeing a book and buying it. The compliment is qualified. But the second is even better. It sounds sarcastic, but it is far more complicated than that.

Elizabeth Solsburg gets my vote for the silver medal with this speech by Delilah:

Sam . . .
I cut your hair while you were asleep.
Forgive me if the short strands
make you feel unmanly and weak.
But it had grown so long
that there was no room
in our bed for me

I thought lines two and three were particularly effective. I also enjoyed this comment by Byron: "Maybe Uncle Sam?"

Millicent Caliban balances humor with truth in a poem that deserves to be published:

We hacked your passwords,
Deleted your documents,
Posted private photos,
And tweeted in your name.
We listened to your calls,
Read all your texts and mails,
Monitored your Facebook likes,
And profiles of friends.
All that we gleaned,
Was passed on to the NSA.
We are so sorry, but you did
Click: "I agree"

I love the movement of Christine Rhein's "Forgive Me," a poem that begins with an echo of William Carlos Williams ("so much depends / upon") and ends "my apology, / your 'well, maybe'." Paul Michelsen reveals his talent for the dramatic monologue in "Hello, Your Honor" and his flair for humor in "My Dearest Love."

I am also crazy about Charise Hoge's wonderful repetition of "list": Forgive me for listing with the wind / and not listening to instructions / – I return the itemized list of how to dwell favorably / beneath the swell of your miniature canopy." Charise also scored with "Butting In": "Sorry, this seat is taken. / You must have mistaken / my husband's lap for a free ride. / Have you no reservations? / Let me help you decide." This is light verse that Dorothy Parker would like.

The last five lines of Angela Ball's "This Is Just to Say" are brilliant, right down to the end note, the mention of the overpriced drug in the news.

This may explain the loud arrival of bees
to which you are highly allergic.
Forgive me, I'm no tragedienne.
I have Munchausen by Proxy
and your last EpiPen.

I hope you won't mind my quoting my own effort. It would not have won this week's first prize.

I borrowed the bottle
of Macallan 18 that you
bought for New Year's
because I knew
you wouldn't mind,
a man as noble as you,
with your refined taste
and fabled generosity.
But tonight is Kol Nidre,
so I repent.

For next week, how about a brief poem entitled "Labor Day." Seven lines or less. It can be an acrostic ("l-i-b-e-r-t-y"), an aphorism, a poem that puns on the multiple meanings of the word "labor," an adieu to summer, an ode to the movie "Picnic" from the point of view of either William Holden or Kim Novak. One rhyme minimum. I think that subject matter generally does not get enough respect, and I believe that the "occasional" poem prompted by a holiday or a birthday is a great little genre.

Deadline: Sunday night, September 4, midnight any time zone.

Again for reasons of space in this book, we are obliged to omit the entries of September 6 through October 11, 2016.

I Stop Somewhere Waiting for You

October 18, 2016

The prompt: to write a brief poem beginning with the last line of Walt Whitman's "Song of Myself." The result: a bounty of poems notable for their excellence and variety. I'm delighted. Kudos to all.

There are six finalists, which I will present in no particular order. Michael C. Rush ("At the Polls") applies the prompt to the election booth. Angela Ball composes a moving eulogy to her "aficionado / of Noir." In Charise Hoge's "Return" the first line ("I stop somewhere waiting for you, / a few paces from reason") returns in inverted form in the ending ("I remember how to decay, a beginning. / I stop waiting for you somewhere.") Ricky Ray's "flowers of memory" yield a "high"; "nose" rhymes with "noise," and the "noble nostrils" that take in the scent teach him the "what of am." The sensuality of Courtney Thrash's poem is fresh. Linda Marie Hilton's "Initials" recall Arthur Rimbaud's "Voyelles" ("Vowels")

Here are the poems:

Return

I stop somewhere waiting for you,
a few paces from reason.
Like the morning glory, I remember
glorifying the gilded blue of new
spreading welcome.
Giddiness overshadowed
by beckoning back to day's end,
by collapse into creases
the sepal skirt that hemmed
me to the skies of us.
I remember how to decay, a beginning.
I stop waiting for you somewhere

Charise Hoge

Poem

I stop somewhere waiting for you;
the grasses are blades in my feet.
clouds stretch out in vain;
a blood-red Sun will not be whitewashed.
I will not leave as I came.
the livestock bleats and bleeds;
I stand naked, rid of Her rags,
in pooling life washed white.
were you ever without your shroud?
the rain falls on seeds and skin bare.
you reap what is sown.
I wait awhile.

Courtney Thrash

Initials

I stop somewhere, waiting for U
Ninth one dotted e.e. writer;
A narrow space, not much tighter
To stand alone, just one of Two.
Some wear a serif, I do not.
I subject U, verb transitive;
I, sole vowel, U action give:
Such gracious length I've always got.
Eyes alight on your fair actions;
U spice my life, you luscious herb:
Against aggression U're my curb;
Eye roll on, having no traction.

Linda Marie Hilton

Noir

I stop somewhere waiting for you,
my aficionado
of Noir:

An honest man is lured
into vice, a squeeze
on the down-low,
murderous insurance.

The night disc-jockey
introduces a number:
his wife and her beau enter
an embrace.

A towering miscreant crashes
in flames—too late
for the good man manqué.

I wait for you under the dark marquee
whose lights have circled
each atom
of our past. Please
catch up.

Angela Ball

Just a Moment

I stop, soul, somewhere, waiting for you
to catch up, and looking back I see
your face buried in the flowers of memory,
your nose deep in the branch inhaling
twenty springs in a snort. How's the high?
Grey winter contaminations? The year half
the sparrows froze and fell? The noise
of them breeding back to their former glory?
Come up, soul, horse, eater of bruises
and apples, I need your ancient nose
to tell me the what of am, your noble
nostrils to remind me that no scent
captures the dog, who, ruff, lingers
over the stain, pays her urine, trots on.

Ricky Ray

At the Polls

I stop somewhere waiting for you
You made promises
I'm somewhere, waiting for you to stop
You promised
I'm waiting for you to stop somewhere
because you promised but didn't deliver
Unable to support yesterday's broken promises
I stop waiting for you and wait for someone
Somewhere to make new promises
But for you, I stop waiting
Here, I stop waiting, and now
I stop

Michael C. Rush

Honorable mention: Paul Michelsen, Berwyn Moore, Patricia Smith, Elizabeth Solsburg.

Who should get the gold? You be the judge. Your job: to write a short poem voting for your choice among the six. Here is how you vote: Use a line from the poem as an epigraph (or in your title; if in the title dedicate the poem to the author). Your poem can but need not make an argument or compare your choice with the other finalists. Fifteen lines or less. Optional: mention Walt Whitman or "Song of Myself" in your poem. Authors of the finalist poems are encouraged to write a poem about a poem not your own.

Deadline: Sunday night, October 23, at midnight in any time zone.

Under the Dark Marquee

October 25, 2016

I feel as if I have guzzled a pot of exquisite espresso in a favorite café, La Victoire in Vence in the Alpes Maritimes or Le Rond Point in Paris. Overstimulated, because of the bounty of wonderful poems—and avid comments—that have filled the comment space of this blog since last Tuesday, when we set upon writing poems inspired by last week's triumphant entries.

First prize this week goes to John Gallaher, whose "I Wait for You under the Dark Marquee" he dedicates to Angela Ball:

The last show before the theater closed down remains,
like a sore throat. It was *The Notebook*. I'm sorry. I'd want it
to be *The Walking Dead*, perhaps, or *Abbott & Costello*
Meet Frankenstein, for the sake of the commuter traffic
passing twice daily, but we get the world we deserve,
not the world we dream of. And now
I hold it in the rearview mirror
as a forced-perspective photograph of a model railroad town
made to look like something we could stand in
as stand-ins for all the things we kept telling ourselves made America great,
some Whitmanesque dream of talking to each other
as if to ourselves. It's the DJ's fault, the songs we end up with,
but then we're the DJ, after all. How'd we forget that?
The four-way stop is dark, but it could be darker, as the marquee
still blinks a little, now and then, as I stop there, waiting for you

I love how this poem, casting its ballot for Angela Ball, concludes with a reprise of the last line of Whitman's "Song of Myself," the prompt that got us started.

Millicent Caliban (who tells us she "loved all six poems," says that Angela's poem "was the one that made [her] write") takes the silver medal for

Under the Dark Marquee
for Angela Ball, aficionado of Noir

You cannot see me, but I am waiting with you
Underneath that dark marquee. Those gaudy circling lights
Are now all gone and we are left without a double feature.
Somewhere else a soulless multiplex has risen,
But we knew how it was to sit together in the dark,
Where we all gasped and felt the frisson
Of the fall to come. Each one of us in thrall
To death, decay, destruction.
We saw the seamy sinews of sin
Encircle the wretched victims,
And knew there could be no compensatory grace.
The films we loved were black and white and Noir.
They told us that the world was full of greed and lust:
Those streets were mean and men were savage, not to trust.
And yet, they also showed that there could be both beauty and regret.

John Findura wins the bronze medal honors for

I Remember How to Decay
for Charise Hoge

After my foot went through
The bottom of the boat
Into the blue-black water
I dried my shoe on the leaves
Of grass wrestling the shoreline
That is where I waited for you
And where you never came
Thoughts, a few, of you
Remind me to fix that boat

And like its deteriorating hull
I remember how to decay
Just like us, I want to tell you,
One syllable at a time

Honorable mention: Anthony DiPietro, whose "I Stand Naked, Rid of Rags" is written in homage to Courtney Thrash):

Battlefield behind me,
full moon above. Ahead my shadow
on barren beach, midnight
blue and white. What saved me
from this last campaign? My dark,
my light, self-worth? A way
with words, alliances,
allegiances? No, surely
not these. I was at play
within inherited wind,
discovered swaying grasses,
pine bark and leaves planted
before my mother's
mother's birth.

Angela Ball, Ricky Ray, and Paul Michelsen are among others who submitted superior work last week.

For next week, what do you say we write seasonal couplets? The only rule: the second line of your couplet should end on the word "leaf," "leave," or "leaves."

Each entry should consist of one couplet, but you are invited to enter as many times as you are moved to do.

Deadline: Sunday, October 30, midnight any time zone.

Leaves of Presence

November 1, 2016

What a plethora of wonderful couplets materialized in response to this week's prompt: a seasonally apt couplet, the only requirement of which is that the second line must end with "leaf," "leaves," or "leave."

I have picked out eight of the couplets and combined them into one collaborative poem, which begins with my own couplet, reflecting my love of wordplay, of songs ("Love Me or Leave Me" with lyrics by Gus Kahn, as sung by Doris Day, and "Greensleeves"), and of Walt Whitman. The second line inverts his title "Leaves of Grass." My untitled effort:

Leave me or love me or sing or singe my green sleeves.
I celebrate my soul, myself, my grass of leaves.

Elizabeth Solsburg's couplet follows, bringing us into the season of mists and mellow fruitfulness:

As daylight shrivels, Autumn weaves
earth's blanket with bright threads of leaves.

Angela Ball dons a Halloween costume:

The Cat Lady, sheathed in fantastic red, was the familiar of phantoms.
Tabbies roiled at her feet; perched in her hair, a lambent leaf.

Wit in the acerb manner of Dorothy Parker is underrated. Note the double meaning of "conceive" in Michael C. Rush's cunning couplet:

Winter's cold, and many cunningly will conceive
a plan for warmth. Next fall—maternity leave!

Paul Michelsen also sets a high value on wit in lines that recollect our original parents and the fig leaves they used after they fell:

According to some theologians we are all Adams and Eves
regardless of how we identify, or what's beneath our leaves.

Daryl Sznyter locates Adam and Eve in the bedroom. Her use of the verb "rake" is noteworthy:

your fitted bed sheets crunch under my hips as you
rake my body like children outside weeping leaves

Jane Keats introduces a strong note of pathos:

Even if you should leave,
would I remain steadfast, and believe?

Finally, our poem ends with the perfect symmetry that Sasha A. Palmer proffers:

Leaves fall
fall leaves

The result is "Grass of Leaves":

Leave me or love me or sing or singe my green sleeves.
I celebrate my soul, myself, my grass of leaves.   *DL*

As daylight shrivels, Autumn weaves
earth's blanket with bright threads of leaves.   *Elizabeth Solsburg*

The Cat Lady, sheathed in fantastic red, was the familiar of phantoms.
Tabbies roiled at her feet; perched in her hair, a lambent leaf.   *Angela Ball*

Winter's cold, and many cunningly will conceive
a plan for warmth. Next fall—maternity leave!   *Michael C. Rush*

According to some theologians we are all Adams and Eves
regardless of how we identify, or what's beneath our leaves.

Paul Michelsen

Your fitted bed sheets crunch under my hips as you
rake my body like children outside weeping leaves.

Daryl Sznyter

Even if you should leave,
would I remain steadfast, and believe?

Jane Keats

Leaves fall
fall leaves.

Sasha A. Palmer

Congratulations to the winners—and heartfelt thanks to all for your ingenuity and skill.

For next week, why don't we take an aphorism by Stanisław Lec ("I prefer the sign 'No Entry' to the one that says 'No Exit'") and use it as the epigraph for a brief poem, ten lines or fewer.

Deadline: Sunday, November 6, midnight any time zone.

No Entry

November 8, 2016

Hamlet was asked whether he considered himself a decisive person. The prince thought for a moment. Then he said, "Yes and no." I feel that way today, reading the many splendid responses that came in to this aphorism by Stanisław Lec: "I prefer the sign 'No Entry' to the one that says 'No Exit.'"

Here are my favorites, in approximate order of preference. From title to closing image, Angela Ball's poem glides brilliantly from hypothetical clauses ("If for you") to affirmations ("we fly ruddy gliders") to future possibilities: "our silk turbans may become / volcanoes."

Don't Come In

I prefer the sign "No Entry" to the one that says "No Exit."
—Stanisław Lec

If for you, women are toy cars
whose wheels you strike
on the ground to make
them go; if for you, women
are tea towels at the feast; if you stand by
as women are swept from the path,
don't approach. In our inviolate
land we fly ruddy gliders;
press oil from impossible fruit; derive power
from waves. At any moment
our silk turbans may become
volcanoes; our shoes,
submarines.

Angela Ball

Charise Hoge's beautiful trapeze simile hooked me, and then there's the magical effect she gets from ending stanza one with "goodbyes" and opening stanza two with "his hello."

Entranced

"I prefer the sign 'No Entry' to the one that says 'No Exit'."—Stanisław Lec

Here he goes showing up
so she's hanging on,
trapped as a trapeze
in swing, between goodbyes.

His hello is wide—
she's soft for a lofty welcome
(unpracticed in soft landings).
He has her in suspense. If
she reads and heeds the signs,
they all shine, 'Going Nowhere.'

Charise Hoge

I admire the sustained metaphor and the closing rhyme in Berwyn Moore's effort (dedicated by the poet to the memory of David Citino and Lucia Perillo):

House of Sclerosis

"I prefer the sign 'No Entry' to the one that says 'No Exit.'"—Stanisław Lec

Gurgling with bourbon, you fall down the stairs
and crack a rib. You laugh yourself to bed.
You nick your chin while shaving and tear
a muscle shooting hoops. When you shred
the cheese and a fingertip, stub your toe,
or scald your tongue, you don't hesitate
to blame the dog, the snow, the squawking crow
or even—clever chef—something you ate.
In time, you shed the scab and pesky limp—

you flee the house of pain. And me? I fall
into atrophied chairs, the light so dim
I can hardly see, the phone dead, the walls
and insulation frayed. I'll take the blame.
I'll stay. The anger here clamors my name.   *Berwyn Moore*

Pat Blake's poem swings from order to chaos and from the light of
the stars to "darkness and / nothingness":

"I prefer the sign 'No Entry' to the one that says 'No Exit'"

It's a commandment
we mostly ignore; we pray
give us this day our daily
order and lead us not into
chaos forever and ever
until the stars cease
to shine, one at a time
leaving darkness and
nothingness alone—until,
at last—no exit   *Pat Blake*

Being a sucker for ingenious wordplay and unusual forms, I responded
davidly, I mean avidly to Sasha A. Palmer's "square poem [which] reads
the same left to right, and top to bottom."

I prefer the sign "No Entry,"
Prefer locked doors to dead ends:
The doors keep trouble under control,
Sign "To Trouble" spells "No Exit."
No, Dead Under No Condition—Rules.
Entry Ends Control, Exit Rules All.   *Sasha A. Palmer*

In Jane Keats's poem, I love the rhymes and the allusions to Sartre's
"No Exit," "Citizen Kane," Genesis, and "Kubla Khan."

"I prefer the sign 'No Entry' to the one that says 'No Exit.'"—S. Lec

Have a heart,
Jean-Paul Sartre.
"No Exit" is hell
Unless you're in Eden
Or in Xanadu,
And Cain—or Kane—is your name
And "No Trespassing" is the sign
Forbidding you
From entering the pleasure dome
That a mogul may call home.

Jane Keats

Anthony DiPietro takes Lec's aphorism and generates four more out of it:

Aphorisms

"I prefer the sign 'No Entry' to the one that says 'No Exit,'" Stanisław Lec

Worry not:
while you sleep,
spiders keep weaving.

What you teach your
children to believe will surely
make them skeptics.

Keep your eyes wide open
and your alcohol close.

Some wear the cloak of politeness,
but kindness goes unclothed.

I made a cento from these seven entries:

For Stanisław Lec

If for you, women are toy cars
or even—clever chef—something you ate,

Angela Ball
Berwyn Moore

give us this day our daily   *Pat Blake*
cloak of politeness   *Anthony DiPietro*
trapped as a trapeze   *Charise Hoge*
that a mogul may call home   *Jane Keats*
preferring locked doors to dead ends.   *Sasha Palmer*

For next week, how about a short poem—eight lines maximum—on either a favorite dish or a favorite drink. The poem can take the form of a recipe, or a memory, or the dish or drink can serve an incidental or decorative purpose. At the urging of a poet friend, I am thinking of writing a poem entitled "Champagne at Night."

Deadline: Sunday night, November 13, midnight any time zone.

The Chill

November 15, 2016

This week's challenge was to write a poem about a favorite or memorable dish or drink.

Millicent Caliban takes first prize with "Revenge," which Charise Hoge characterizes as "beautifully biting":

To begin with, take a few perceived slights,
Add some social put downs or jokes at your expense.
Sprinkle in any recollected barbed comments
With gratuitous insults. Mix well.
Simmer slowly for a long time
In a sauce concocted of bile and bad blood.
Baste frequently and season with bitter herbs.
Layer this mixture over stinging nettles.
Now make a topping of seeming sweetness—
Honeyed words work well—and smooth it over
But only on the surface. Garnish generously with grapes of wrath.
Chill thoroughly and serve cold (while smiling).

The recipe form, with its sequence of imperatives, is perfect, as are the alliteration ("seeming sweetness," "bile and bad blood," the choice phrases ("bitter herbs") and the brilliant parenthetical close.

The silver medal goes to Elizabeth Solsburg's poem that treats the same "classic dish best served cold":

We've swallowed raw lye that scalds our throats,
poison dissolving our souls
like the liquid flesh of squash split
and rotting in a field where it sits

too long—we scrabble for an icy antidote,
the classic dish best served cold
There's a plate already chilling;
be quick, we are ravening.

To which Millicent Caliban replied, in a comment, "I like your oblique approach to our mutual dish as an 'antidote.' We both know how to serve it."

Of the many other worthy poems that came in—including recipes and rhymes, a multipart abecedarius and "erasures" of certain notable poems—I was charmed most by Angela Ball's **"Kahiki Polynesian Supper Club, Columbus, 1971."** The poem is based on a memory in which "a hollowed pineapple, sweet-sour / chicken" plays an incidental part:

Kahiki Polynesian Supper Club, Columbus, 1971

Its sacred goddess drew us, waving
from her billboard, her spell
dictating we wait two hours
to dine in the company
of flaming torches and signed glossies:
Bob Hope, Bing Crosby, Dorothy Lamour.
My dish a hollowed pineapple, sweet-sour
chicken—the most sophistication
I'd ever tasted. Ripe for conquest by the glamour
known to Hope (an Ohio native!)
and the rest, primed to claim its totems
for my own, I reveled, oblivious
to the dark charade
of Asian waitresses wrapped
and knotted in strategic batik,
who were—according to the restaurant's brochure—
the "wives of servicemen
from Japan or Korea," all rigidly
trained, unused
to this kind of work."

In an exchange with the indefatigable Paul Michelsen, Angela clarified that the place she describes can be seen online. "Really pretty amazing. It was probably the only Tiki Bar on the Register of Historic Places—until a Walgreen's, under protest, tore it down." Among the drinks served there, Paul reported, were "Blue Hurricane," "Instant Urge," "Maiden's Prayer," and "The Smoking Eruption."

While I had something else in mind for next week, I am going to postpone the idea and suggest instead that we write poems entitled "Blue Hurricane," "Instant Urge," "Maiden's Prayer," or "The Smoking Eruption." The poem can but need not have anything to do with a cocktail.

Deadline: Sunday, November 20, midnight any time zone.

Honor Role of Weekly Winners

2014

May 13: Leo Braudy
May 20: Brian Anderson's twelfth-grade class
May 27: Frank Bidart
June 3: MQ
June 10: Anna E. Moss
June 17: Lewis Saul
June 24: Diana Ferraro
July 1: James the Lesser
July 8: Jamie
July 15: Sandra M. Gilbert
July 22: MQ
July 29: Katie Whitney
August 5: Laura Cronk
August 19: Paul Breslin
August 26: Barbara Shine
October 21: Bruce Bond
October 28: Tara
November 18: Jennifer Clarvoe
December 2: Kempy Bloodgood
December 16: Rebecca Epstein

2015

January 13: Nin Andrews, Rachel Barenblat
January 27: Diane Seuss
February 3: Angela Ball
February 10: Charise Hoge
February 17: James the Lesser
February 24: Angela Ball, Rachel Barenblat, James the Lesser, Paul Michelsen, Charise Hoge, Christine Rhein
March 3: Angela Ball
March 10: Patricia Smith
March 17: Paul Michelsen
March 31: Howard Altmann, Christine Rhein
April 14: Paul Michelsen
April 21: Berwyn Moore
April 28: Patricia Smith
May 5: Jennifer Clarvoe
May 19: Angela Ball, Charise Hoge, Christine Rhein
June 2: Paul Michelsen, LaWanda Walters
June 16: Millicent Caliban, Christine Rhein
June 30: Patricia Smith
July 7: Annette Boehm, Paul Michelsen
July 14: Christine Rhein
July 21: Charise Hoge
July 28: Berwyn Moore
August 4: Jordan Sanderson
August 11: Patricia Smith
August 18: Jordan Sanderson
August 25: Berwyn Moore
September 1: Patricia Smith
September 8: Jordan Sanderson
September 15: Patricia Smith
September 22: Berwyn Moore
September 29: Paul Michelsen
October 13: Michael C. Rush
October 20: Angela Ball
October 27: Christine Rhein

November 3: Elizabeth Solsburg
November 10: Christine Rhein
November 17: Patricia Smith
November 24: Paul Michelsen
December 1: Poem Today
December 8: Angela Ball
December 15: Berwyn Moore
December 22: Joe Lawlor
December 29: Brandon Crist

2016

January 5: Charise Hoge
January 12: Millicent Caliban, Paul Michelsen, Elizabeth Solsburg,
January 26: Angela Ball
February 2: Elizabeth Solsburg
February 9: Paul Michelsen
February 16: Angela Ball, Charise Hoge, Patricia Smith
February 23: Berwyn Moore
March 1: Carey James
March 8: Angela Ball, Millicent Caliban, Sarah Paley
March 22: Eduardo Ramos Ruiz
March 29: Angela Ball, Dick Humbird, Eduardo Ramos Ruiz, Karen Topham
April 5: Millicent Caliban, Paul Michelsen
April 12: Beth Gylys
April 19: Pat Blake, Millicent Caliban
April 26: Millicent Caliban
May 3: Angela Ball
May 10: Millicent Caliban
May 17: Angela Ball
May 24: Paul Michelsen
June 7: Millicent Caliban
August 23: Millicent Caliban, Berwyn Moore
August 30: Marissa D'Espain
October 18: Angela Ball, Linda Marie Hilton, Charise Hoge, Ricky Ray,
    Michael C. Rush, Courtney Thrash
October 25: John Gallaher

November 1: Angela Ball, Jane Keats, Paul Michelsen, Sasha A. Palmer,
   Michael C. Rush, Elizabeth Solsburg, Daryl Sznyter
November 8: Angela Ball
November 15: Millicent Caliban

Note: To explain the gaps in dates: No honors were given on certain weeks when a prompt was announced and explained. There were also one or two holiday weeks. Nineteen posts were omitted for reasons of space. Some "Next Line, Please" regulars won those contests. Other winners, unacknowledged in the list above, include Amanda J. Bradley, Joel Carrera, Rebecca Morgan Frank, Leonard Kress, Hans Ostrom, and Willard Spiegelman.

Angela Ball wrote the entries from June 23, 2015, through September 29, 2015; David Lehman composed the rest.

Index

CPSIA information can be obtained
at www.ICGtesting.com
Printed in the USA
LVOW03s0216030218

565167LV00001B/62/P

9 781501 715006